# Mother Teresa

# MOTHER TERESA

## *The Early Years*

\* \* \*

David Porter

First published in Great Britain 1986
SPCK
Holy Trinity Church
Marylebone Road
London NW1 4DU

British Library Cataloguing in Publication Data

Porter, David, *1945–*
  Mother Teresa: the early years.
  1. Teresa, *Mother*  2. Nuns—India—Calcutta
  —Biography
  I. Title
  266′.2′0924      BX4705.T4455

ISBN 0–281–04189–X

Filmset by Northumberland Press Ltd, Gateshead
Printed in Great Britain by
Richard Clay (The Chaucer Press) Ltd, Bungay, Suffolk

# Contents

# Foreword

David Porter's contribution to the literature relating to Mother Teresa deals with her childhood and young-womanhood in Albania – a phase in her life that has been hardly noticed. Mother Teresa, it goes without saying, has little taste for writing or talking about herself; she considers that whatever she may achieve is but a gift from God, about which she must be thankful but not vociferous. Fortunately, David Porter has had access to translations of Albanian writings about Mother Teresa, especially her brother Lazar's memories of their growing up together.

Mother Teresa's fame, rightly spread throughout the world, is based on her illimitable concern for homeless people, abandoned children, lepers, the dying, all who are in distress – as she always puts it, 'the poorest of the poor'. David Porter explores how the seeds of this were in a loving home, a Christian upbringing and a readiness to pick up her cross and follow Jesus. As a child Mother Teresa was, it seems, good at her studies and devout at her prayers; already conscious that some special mission would be required of her, and preparing herself to undertake it. This involved leaving her home to become a nun in the Loreto Order in Ireland, then a teacher at a Loreto school in Calcutta, before venturing alone into appalling Calcutta slums to live with and care for the poor there, ultimately founding her own Order, the Missionaries of Charity.

The picture of Mother Teresa in her youthfulness that emerges in this book shows her as being like every normal young girl, full of delight in life and in the prospect of motherhood and her own home. And we wonder at her putting all this aside, in her exclusive dedication to the poor. Likewise with her public words: ordinary enough, yet they hold every audience spellbound. I can never forget her address in Cambridge after receiving an honorary degree; when she spoke of love and compassion, it was as though words were coming direct from heaven – as, indeed, I'm sure they were.

It has long seemed to me that whatever our collective plight on earth may be, God always sends us saints to help us. There seems to be no doubt whatsoever that Mother Teresa has been cast in this role, though she herself is quite unaware of it. As the scientists struggle on from bomb to bomb, from transplant to transplant, the religious orders pine for postulants – whereas Mother Teresa is overwhelmed by them. Because she claims nothing she finds everything; like St Francis of Assisi whom she greatly admires, and whose words she often quotes, she manages to possess nothing and to ask for nothing, and yet to have everything that enables her to go on looking after and loving the poorest of the poor.

Malcolm Muggeridge

# Preface

Any writer adding to the wealth of words written about Mother Teresa of Calcutta needs to have good reasons for doing so, especially as she herself has always shunned the limelight.

My own interest in Mother Teresa was first aroused, as it was for so many, by the work of Malcolm Muggeridge, whose film *Something Beautiful For God* was followed by a luminous and compelling book with the same title. When later I wrote a book about Malcolm Muggeridge, I was impressed by the influence Mother Teresa had clearly had upon him and the enormous warmth with which he speaks of her. Through meeting him I sensed that I was meeting her and, at a sort of third hand, meeting the Lord himself.

In 1984 I was invited by SPCK to work on the editing of a translation of Lush Gjergji's *Mother Teresa: the First Complete Biography*. Gjergji is an Albanian priest and journalist, a cousin of Mother Teresa, and his main reason for writing was to give Albanians an account of their most distinguished Christian sister. The project was approved by Mother Teresa herself. She saw it, characteristically, as a means of glorifying God. The book was indeed the first complete biography of her published in the Albanian language.

Gjergji interviewed many people in the Balkans and spent considerable time with Lazar, her brother. He was able to visit places and individuals that had been significant in the early life of Mother Teresa. For the later part of the story he relied heavily on other published accounts, though again he was able to provide some unique material on her contacts with her family, her homeland and her home church.

His book was translated into several languages, and when the opportunity arose for a British edition it was accepted with interest. However, for a number of reasons, it became evident that it would not be possible to publish Gjergji's work in its entirety in Britain, and it was also very apparent that knowledge of many aspects of the Albanian and Yugoslavian background had been taken for granted by the author – who was in any case writing primarily for people of those nationalities.

The present book is therefore aimed at making available to a British readership the material assembled by the original author, much of which could never be gathered again. It is based heavily on Gjergji's work, which it simultaneously abridges and expands, and concentrates on the early years of Mother Teresa because that is the part of her life on which he had the most interesting things to say. The fascinating and unique photographs are provided by the original publishers.

I have expanded much of the original, added background material, an epilogue, many comments of my own, and explanatory sections; and I have checked those areas where Gjergji did not have access to research resources. It ought to be pointed out, however, that

Mother Teresa's interest in her own biography is minimal, and she has not been able to keep accurate records.

I hope very much that this book will have a part in the work of letting people know what Mother Teresa is doing. My reason for adding yet another to the books that have been written about her is that so little has been compiled about her early life; yet it is a remarkable story. It is not a sensational epic. It explodes no myths. It gives no earth-shaking revelations. The story of Mother Teresa's childhood and youth is, quite simply, a demonstration of how God can take the life of any individual who is willing to offer it to him, and make of it something quite literally superhuman in its power and its effectiveness. This is a story of the making of a child of God.

An outline of Mother Teresa's work after the 1960s is given for the sake of completeness, but full accounts are best given by people intimately associated with the work. I have made good use of three such authors: Kathryn Spink, *For the Brotherhood of Man Under the Fatherhood of God* (Colour Library International 1981); Desmond Doig, *Mother Teresa: Her People and Her Work* (Collins 1976); and E. Le Joly, *We Do It For Jesus* (Darton, Longman and Todd 1977). I have also used some of the small collections of her meditations and prayers which have been published.

Several people have been extremely helpful to me, and I would like to thank particularly Sister Immacula of the Loreto Sisters in St Albans, and Rod and Carolyn Nelson who shared with me their recollections of Calcutta. From a long reading list of books I have consulted apart from those about Mother Teresa, I would single out Bishop

Stephen Neill's monumental and incomparably readable *History of Christian Missions* (Penguin Books 1964).

David Porter
May 1985

# 1
# ORIGINS

The young nun smiled at the couple standing expectantly in front of her. The old man had an infectious laugh. His nose had been broken at some time and had set again crookedly. An impressive moustache drooped below it, merging into a long beard. His eyes blinked cheerfully as he spoke.

'For myself I want nothing at all,' he declared. He indicated the woman at his side, standing forlornly, a look of mute suffering on her face. She was short, like him, and very attractive. 'Her ears hurt,' he explained. He pushed her forward and she bent her head obediently as the nun examined the painful ears. Behind, the queue of waiting patients shuffled forward to take up the vacant place.

A quick glance confirmed that the woman's ears were clogged with wax and dirt. The nun looked at the man. 'I must clean them,' she said. He nodded and winked, and took the woman's arm. A look of dismay passed over her face. The nun indicated the 'operating table' – an old packing-case which, scrubbed clean, served as a low bench.

When she caught sight of it and saw the gleaming syringe being prepared, the woman leapt back in alarm.

After some vigorous argument from her companion she was eventually persuaded to return to the bench, where she stood glowering, raising first one leg and then the other in an attempt to step up on to it. Some of the waiting patients proffered advice and noisy encouragement.

The nun stepped forward and spoke quietly to the woman. 'You do not need to stand up on it. Just sit down. Do not try to get up on it.' The woman shook her head worriedly and continued her efforts.

The old man shrugged his shoulders, sat down heavily on the bench, folded his arms and glared at the woman. 'Do this!' he shouted. The woman obeyed. The man beamed at the young nun. 'You see, she has never sat on anything higher than the ground itself,' he explained.

When the woman's ears had been cleaned, other people came forward for treatment. Mothers pushed their children in front and waited anxiously while the infants were examined. The children's backs were covered in pustules the size of small fists. These had to be lanced, the infection scraped clean, and the wounds bandaged; the same painstaking routine multiplied many times. Of all the sicknesses that brought people to the mission for treatment, this kind of infection was the most common.

A woman called out from the queue. 'Hey, Catholic Mother! My husband didn't want me to come here at any price. He said the barber could operate on my child.' The woman grinned triumphantly. 'So I said to him, "I'm taking the child to Mother!" – and I rushed out!'

Mother Teresa of Calcutta smiled briefly and carried on with her work.

Today the work of Mother Teresa is known and honoured throughout the world. Her Missionaries of Charity operate in many countries among the poor and the outcast. She has been the subject of widespread attention in books, and on radio and television. Yet she continues today exactly as she did before, carrying out her vocation to serve Christ by serving the poorest of the poor.

A great deal has been written about her work, but very little about her more personal early life. She wants her work to be known only for two reasons: the needs of the poor, and that people should be wakened to the fact that their Lord suffers in the suffering of the weak, the oppressed and the destitute; and she has built her work on the concept of 'Co-workers' – people all over the world who, because they have read or heard about her work, have committed themselves to bearing the sacrificial burden of prayer which is central to all that the Missionaries of Charity are doing.

The woman who is known throughout the world as 'Mother Teresa' was born in 1910 in Skopje in Serbia. One of three children, she was given the name Ganxhe Agnes Bojaxhiu. Her parents were Albanian. For one whose work was to be honoured with the highest awards for peace, it was an unlikely time and place in which to begin life.

Agnes Bojaxhiu was born into a world teetering on the brink of war and she spent her childhood in its shadow. The year 1910 witnessed the first Albanian Rising. Two years later the first Balkan War broke out. In 1914 Europe was thrown into the turmoil of the Great War, one of the causes of which was the unrest in the Balkan States.

Within Serbia and neighbouring Albania there was internal fighting, and when Albania achieved independence in 1912 Serbia resented losing its hopes of a coastline – hopes to be satisfied only when Yugoslavia was created as a federation of Serbia and five other States. The lives of the Bojaxhius, whose roots were in both countries, reflected the times. Agnes's father, Kole Bojaxhiu, was a successful merchant with political interests who sympathized with the Albanian patriots and gave them financial support and hospitality.

He often entertained his patriot friends. He loved to sit late into the night in their company, exchanging dreams of the bright future of Albania or arguing politics with tenacity and enormous enthusiasm – sometimes in one of the four foreign languages which he had learned in the course of his business. The house in Skopje often rang with songs of war and rebellion, and numerous photographs and other mementoes around the house were a constant reminder of 'The Cause'.

In November 1912 Albania achieved its independence and Kole hosted a gathering in his home to mark the long-desired occasion. It was a celebrated assembly. Curri was there, the famous fighter against the Turks who had controlled Albania for centuries, and others such as Hasan Prishtina and Sabri Qytezi who were also revered among patriots. All night long the patriots talked, and sang songs of victory to the traditional accompaniment of a mandoline.

Agnes's brother Lazar, then four years old, watched solemnly as matchboxes heaped in the centre of the room were set alight. The memory of the victory flames leaping to the ceiling stayed with him until his death.

Kole Bojaxhiu was a prosperous merchant of the type that has flourished in Europe for centuries. He came from Albanian merchant stock, a large, long-established family with business interests extending as far as Egypt (the name is derived from *boja*, meaning 'colour', and may indicate that the Bojaxhius once traded in paints). The Bojaxhius originally came from Prizren, a city in what is now southern Yugoslavia and was once a region of the kingdom of Serbia. It is the sort of city where merchants settle. An important trading centre in medieval times, in the fourteenth century it became the capital city of Serbia. Today it produces filigree-silver jewellery, carpets and fine embroidery.

In the middle of the nineteenth century an outbreak of cholera struck Prizren and its population was decimated. That may have been the reason why the family was dispersed; but there is another belief that the reason was Turkish persecution, especially of those living in the old city. It has been suggested also that it was the search for new markets that drove the family on. Whatever the reason, many of the Bojaxhius moved to other places. While some remained in Prizren, some went to Scutari on the Albanian border, where in 1930 Kole's son discovered a street named Bojaxhiu Street and met an old woman who remembered the family well. Other members of the family settled in the ancient city of Skopje on the Vardar river.

Like Prizren, Skopje was an attractive city for a merchant family. Its history goes back to Roman and Byzantine times. In the thirteenth century it was captured by the Serbs, but a century later the city fell to the Turks.

It remained under Turkish influence until recaptured by the Serbs in the Balkan Wars during Agnes's early childhood.

Among the Bojaxhius who came to Skopje was Kole. As soon as he arrived in the city he bought a house. A self-made man with brilliant entrepreneurial flair, he worked at first with a doctor, Suskalovic, selling medicine. Suskalovic was one of the most eminent doctors in Skopje, and Kole acquired a local reputation as a pharmacist. But pharmacy was never his ambition and it was not long before he grasped the chance of becoming a partner with a friend who was in the building trade. The partnership flourished and the firm prospered. At the time of his death Kole owned several houses, in one of which Agnes, her sister and her brother, grew up.

It was a wealthy background to a comfortable childhood. Agnes's grandmother on her father's side, a woman of exceptional gifts in both craftmanship and management, ran an embroidery business which employed a large number of workers. She and her husband had built up the family fortunes considerably before handing them on to Kole.

The life of a prosperous merchant was a busy one. As Agnes grew into childhood, her father was often away from home. Soon he had acquired new business interests. He met an Italian, Signor Morten, a very wealthy merchant who traded in a wide range of luxury goods: foodstuffs, oil, sugar, cloth, leather. He and Kole agreed to go into partnership. So Bojaxhiu began to travel all over Europe, buying and selling.

The three Bojaxhiu children – Agnes, her older sister

Aga and her brother Lazar – treasured the moments when a coach laden with parcels would draw up outside their home in Skopje, signifying that Kole Bojaxhiu, property-owner and prosperous merchant, was home from his travels again.

In old age, Lazar Bojaxhiu recalled those times with affection. The presents from foreign countries were exciting, but what the children looked forward to most when their father came home were his reports of what he had been doing. Kole was a wonderful storyteller and entertained his family for hours with uproarious accounts of what had taken place while he was abroad.

Kole Bojaxhiu seems to have been a mixture of jollity and severity. On the one hand, the children could often lie in bed listening to the laughter and song when he was entertaining the patriots; but he was also, according to Lazar, a severe disciplinarian who had high expectations of his children.

He took a keen interest in their education. His friends and neighbours considered him a man of very progressive ideas – to educate two daughters as well as a son was an achievement in those difficult times. Often he would come home in the evening and go up to Lazar's bedroom, where he would wake his son to demand whether he had been a good boy at school that day. He also regularly examined him in the subjects he was studying in class.

Agnes and Lazar loved their father but seem to have stood rather in awe of him, while Aga had a special place in his affection. He strove to teach all his children habits of discipline, urging them: 'Never forget whose children you are!'

7

In all this the Bojaxhiu household and its head were no different from many well-to-do Skopje families of that time, while in England Lazar's contemporaries in families of similar social standing were calling their fathers 'Sir' and children were well used to severe discipline and an emphasis on obedience and manners.

The priests and dignitaries of the Church were frequent visitors, and Kole contributed generously to Christian work in the parish. The clergy who visited often expressed their gratitude: 'Kole, may God reward you for your kindness!' Though he was constantly travelling and was not always at home, his family knew that he was a committed Christian and that the Church was very close to his heart.

He was a generous man, who distributed food and money to many people without drawing attention to the fact; and his son often received parcels of money, clothes and food together with instructions that they were to be given to the poor. His door was always open to those who needed food, shelter and care. Kole was especially fond of an old woman who was regularly welcomed into the Bojaxhiu home for her meals. 'Welcome her lovingly,' he commanded his children. He taught his family as strictly about the need for generosity and compassion as he did about the need to work hard at school. He often admonished Agnes, while she was very young, 'My daughter, never take a morsel of food that you are not prepared to share with others.'

Kole Bojaxhiu's robust sense of the responsibilities of wealth was complemented by that of his wife, Drana. She was a local girl in Prizren when he married her. Her mother had been a merchant and landowner, and her family owned large estates in Serbia.

Drana was an indomitable woman of great strength of character, generous and hardworking. These qualities were greatly needed in the home in Skopje, for when Agnes was only eight years old Kole Bojaxhiu, the strict but much-loved father of the three young children, died.

He had been to Belgrade with his fellow city councillors to attend a meeting and, while there, he was taken gravely ill. He arrived home in the early evening, having been brought in a carriage by the Italian consul. He was rushed to hospital where the next morning he underwent an emergency operation. It was unsuccessful. The following day, he died.

The private grief of the family was echoed in the city's sadness at the loss of one of its most celebrated characters and public figures. Kole had become part of Skopje's civic and cultural life – with Morten, he had been responsible for the building of its first theatre – and he had been a man of wide interests and many charities.

Large crowds attended the funeral. Official delegates came from the city council, on which he had been the only Catholic councillor, but other religions were well represented. On the day of the funeral every jeweller's shop in Skopje was closed. The pupils in all the city's schools received commemorative handkerchiefs, in keeping with a local tradition observed on such occasions. The number of handkerchiefs given away was an indication of the wealth of the person who had died, and of the standing of his family.

# 2

# DRANA

When Kole died, his children were still young. Aga, whom her father had often called 'my right hand', was only fifteen years old; Lazar was eleven, and Agnes eight. It was a time of hardship as well as grief, especially for Drana Bojaxhiu. The whole burden of looking after the house, managing the family finances and educating the three children fell on her shoulders. She resolutely decided to make sure that, so far as it was possible, the rest of their childhood should be untroubled.

The death of Kole meant that the life of the family changed dramatically. Drana was determined that the children should not be deprived, and that meant that she had to find work. For a time she had an income from Kole's business, but eventually Morten brought his commercial relationship with the family to an end. She then took up sewing and embroidery, making fine clothes, wedding dresses, and costumes for wearing at feasts and festivals.

She was a woman of extraordinary character. Although her family owned large estates in Novi Selo, she could not benefit from them. The parish priest of that region asked Lazar several times: 'Why does your mother not take an interest in the family property?' But when he raised the matter with Drana she explained that there was some dispute within her family as to whom the estates belonged, and she possessed no documents establishing her rights. It would have crushed a woman of lesser character, but Drana accepted the situation philosophically and worked at her embroidery.

For Agnes it must have been a powerful example of how a Christian handles disappointment and assesses the importance to be placed on worldly possessions. Drana had been the wife of a prosperous, respected citizen. Her home had been famous for its parties and hospitality. Now, though she was poorer, her home was still famous for the important things: kindness, gentleness, generosity and compassion towards the poor.

Her faith was very deep, and central to her life. She brought her children up to live disciplined lives, but imposed few rules on them. She preferred to set them a good example and required them to be examples in their turn. 'She always told us', Lazar recalled, 'that we should ask her for anything we wanted. But she said that she would expect something of us in return; that we would be good children and an example to others.'

She also taught them the priceless lesson of pratical, personal piety. Every evening the family prayed together, and their life was centred on the Church – not only in its daily acts of worship but in its calendar of festivals and celebrations.

Like other Christian families of Skopje they venerated the Madonna of Letnice, whose shrine had been built in the mountainous region of Montenegro. Letnice was a beloved place for which the worshippers had an intense and almost childlike devotion, and the highlight of each year was the pilgrimage across the mountains to the shrine. Parties of people travelled together, praying and singing on the road. The Bojaxhius went in a horse-drawn carriage, though Aga and Agnes usually made the journey to Letnice several weeks before the pilgrimage and stayed there for the benefit of Agnes's health. She was a frail child, susceptible to malaria and whooping cough; for her sake the family often took their holidays at Vrnjacka Banja, which was famous throughout Yugoslavia for its thermal springs. But each year at Letnice, away from the city and in an environment that she found spiritually refreshing, she regained her strength.

When the two girls went ahead to Letnice, Aga received strict instructions from her mother to take Agnes for long walks, to see that she had adequate rest and not allow her to read too much: left to her own devices, Agnes would have happily buried her head in a book for the whole day.

At Letnice they often stayed in a house which had been provided for their use. It belonged to a local man and Kole Bojaxhiu had helped him build it. Out of gratitude the owner placed the house at their disposal every year. The visits to Letnice were among the happiest times of Agnes's childhood, when the family spent all day together, playing games, going for walks near the Letnice springs, and in the evenings sitting around the fireside, laughing and telling stories into the small hours.

Agnes looked forward to the pilgrimage every year. Though she was not strong, she was not withdrawn by nature. Her Christianity was very important to her, and she loved the Church and its festivals as much for the fellowship with her family and other believers as for anything else. Crowds of people made their way to Letnice annually to bear witness to their faith; not only Catholics, but Christians of many other traditions.

She attended church joyfully and often quietly took her place when no one else was there. She liked to pray on her own and was often to be found kneeling before the statue of the Sacred Heart of Jesus. (In the Skopje earthquake of 1963 the church of the Sacred Heart of Jesus was destroyed but the statue was saved and remains there to this day.)

Though devotion and worship were central in the life of the Bojaxhiu family, their Christianity had many practical outworkings. The children grew up with an awareness of the needs of the poor. Mother Teresa has recalled:

> Many of the poor in and around Skopje knew our house, and none left it empty-handed. We had guests at table every day. At first I used to ask, 'Who are they?', and Mother would answer: 'Some are relatives, but all of them are our people.' When I was older, I realized that the strangers were poor people who had nothing and whom my mother was feeding.

Drana Bojaxhiu was certain that anything she gave to the poor, she was giving to God. She taught this to her children. 'When you do good,' she told them, 'do it unobtrusively, as if you were tossing a pebble into the sea.' In Calcutta and in other countries today, the foundation laid by Drana still undergirds the work of the Missionaries of Charity. Mother Teresa teaches all her

Sisters that they must seek no reward or recognition for their work; and that when they wash away the filth and dress the wounds of a beggar, they are ministering to the sufferings and wounds of Christ.

Drana gave her daughters plenty of practical training in helping others. There were many who needed their help. Once a week, often accompanied by Agnes, Drana visited an elderly woman who had been abandoned by her son. She brought food and cleaned the house.

Another woman who received regular visits from the Bojaxhius was File, an alcoholic who was covered in sores and very ill. Twice a day Drana washed File and cared for her, and often Agnes helped her.

Yet another who looked forward to visits from Drana was a widow whose health was failing and who was struggling to bring up six children. When Drana was not able to visit her, she sent Agnes, and when the widow died the children were welcomed into the Bojaxhiu home as part of the family.

For a young girl who would one day find herself ministering to the needs of the dying, the destitute and the physically deformed, it was an object lesson in love. Drana had no concept of 'charity' except in its original sense of 'care'. She moved among the dirty and the physically repellent, washing their bodies and tending their wounds, and she treated each person as a unique individual. Though many of those she helped were destitute, she welcomed them all with joy.

So Agnes received her first lessons in caring – her first missionary training – in the environment of her family home. It is perhaps not surprising that her brother, as an old man, considered that she had the same qualities of character and faith as their mother. When she herself was grown up, talking about her decision to become a missionary nun, she remarked that the only problem had been that it meant leaving her home, which had been an exceptionally happy one. 'We were a family full of joy and love, and we children were happy and contented.'

# 3
# PARISH PRIESTS

It is a strange contradiction in the Christian life that individuals should become celebrated and honoured for their faith and their works. The New Testament is very explicit on the matter. Believers are urged not to draw attention to their good deeds. Matthew records in his Gospel that Jesus reserved for the scribes and Pharisees – notorious public do-gooders – some of his most savage criticism and that he urged his followers to do their works of charity away from the public gaze.

Mother Teresa has consistently rejected any personal fame or reward for her work. She has said repeatedly that what is important is not her personal achievement or any sacrifice she and her Sisters might have made, but the work of God of whom she is an instrument. When in 1979 she was honoured with the award of the Nobel Peace Prize, her reaction was characteristic: 'Personally, I am unworthy. I accept it gratefully in the name of the poor.'

It might be reasonably argued that just as Mother Teresa has taught the world some important lessons on Christian attitudes to failure, destitution and poverty, so she has also taught us valuable lessons about the correct handling of success and recognition.

But it remains true that God has made his work through the Missionaries of Charity something of world-wide interest. Mother Teresa has a secure place in the history of modern Christianity. That fame has become an instrument of spreading the work of the Kingdom of God throughout the world. Wherever people have heard of Mother Teresa, they have been forced to think about their responsibility towards their own poor.

It is a remarkable thing that when one looks closely at the life of someone who has been given prominence in this way, almost always it becomes clear that one or more hardly-remembered individuals played a profound part in the spiritual growth of that person. Great workers for God do not spring fully-formed on to the stage of history. He prepares the way by providing teachers, leaders, friends and other supporters. The Bible is full of examples of this, and so is the long history of the Christian Church. And the life of Mother Teresa is no exception.

Of all the influences upon young Agnes Bojaxhiu, the strongest was certainly her family. In the example of her father and mother she saw kindness and compassion at first hand. They did not spare her the sight of human need and poverty, though it would have been easy for them to do so. On the contrary, they invited the poor into their home and made them welcome.

After the example of her family, the second major influence on Agnes was the Church. 'Though we went to state schools,' she has said, 'my family, and later the parish priest, gave me a sound and thorough religious education.'

Her family had been Catholics for generations. In the Balkan States Roman Catholicism was a minority faith: in Albania, where the family originated, the Catholic population even in the years before the wars was never more than ten per cent of the whole, and the majority of the population was Muslim. In Serbia, Catholics were also in a minority. For centuries the majority of Serbs had followed the Orthodox faith. Neighbouring Croatia was predominantly Roman Catholic, but between the two states throughout history there had been a great deal of bitterness, and it is still to be found today.

The Catholic community in Skopje was a minority community and had no close contacts with other members of the Roman Communion. Until 1914 Skopje was an archdiocese with a Catholic population scattered over a wide area. Even today there are only a few thousand Catholic believers living in the modern city, which was rebuilt in 1963 after the earthquake that year had virtually destroyed the city in which Agnes grew up. They live in a society of over half a million people, now primarily atheistic, with some Orthodox and Muslim citizens.

In the early twentieth century Catholic churches and priests in the archdiocese were few and far between. Spiritual life suffered in consequence. In 1909 a new archbishop arrived in Skopje: Lazer Mjeda. He was a realist. He had not been long in the city before he came to the conclusion that if the Church were to move forward, it would only be with help from outside. He approached the Venetian Jesuit missionaries, and in 1910 a Jesuit house was opened in the city, in the home of a local poet.

The Catholic church in Skopje was quite near to the

Bojaxhiu home and Mjeda was often a visitor. Agnes soon became familiar with the famous preacher and his dynamic personality. Kole was a personal friend of the archbishop, and this made him even more generous towards the church than he would naturally have been.

But Mjeda did not stay in Skopje for long. Overshadowed by the threat of war in the Balkans, he and his Jesuit colleagues struggled with the problems of the small and scattered community. As the political situation worsened, the work of the archdiocese became increasingly difficult. When the Balkan War finally broke out in 1912, the Jesuits had to confine their work to the city. In 1914 the First World War began, and a difficult situation became desperate when Mjeda was removed by his superiors to Skadar to become the new metropolitan archbishop.

His place was taken by Toma Glasnovic, who was already working in the archdiocese and who was also a regular visitor to Agnes's home. Glasnovic took a long look at the city parish of Skopje and embarked on a programme of radical remedy. Like Mjeda, he realized that outside help was vital. He wrote to a large number of religious authorities in Serbia, without success. Finally he wrote to the Provincial in Zagreb and obtained permission for the Jesuits to take over the running of the parish of the Sacred Heart in Skopje.

So it was that in 1921, when Agnes Bojaxhiu was eleven years old, Fr Gasper Zadrima arrived as parish priest at the church of the Sacred Heart of Jesus. The Bojaxhiu children, who had known both his predecessors as family friends, contemplated the new arrival with mixed feelings.

He was a hard worker, an Albanian who spoke fluent Serbo-Croat. With this background he was able to identify with most of his scattered parishioners and understand many of their problems, and he rapidly established himself in the community. On the other hand, he was a strict disciplinarian who demanded order and good behaviour. During church services he carried a thick walking-stick, which his young parishioners eyed with some apprehension, though it is not recorded that he ever used it for anything more violent than beating time. Agnes quietly observed the new priest. One day she challenged her brother: 'I have the feeling that you are not very keen on Father Zadrima.'

'How do you expect me to like him,' retorted Lazar, 'when he is always swinging that enormous stick?'

'Even so,' Agnes replied thoughtfully, 'it is your duty to love him and give him respect. He is Christ's priest.'

In later life, that same attitude of Mother Teresa towards the authority and discipline of the Church and its appointed leaders profoundly impressed Malcolm Muggeridge. 'Ecclesiastical authority', he wrote, '... is something that she accepts in the same unquestioning way that peasants accept the weather, or sailors storms at sea. It would never occur to her to venerate it or to challenge it.'

Before long Father Zadrima was given an assistant, a priest who had a flair for organization. He helped with the work among children and young people, but he could hardly speak Albanian and this was a problem. He found particular difficulty in conducting catechism classes.

1. *The Bojaxhiu family were all musical. Agnes's father, Kole, was a member of Skopje's band (March 1912).*

2. *Agnes at ten years old, with friends in Skopje.*

1. *The Bojaxhiu family were all musical. Agnes's father, Kole, was a member of Skopje's band (March 1912).*

2. *Agnes at ten years old, with friends in Skopje.*

3. As a primary school pupil, taking part in a Christmas Eve play, Skopje 1924.

4. *Agnes (right) with brother Lazar and sister Aga, 1924.*

5. Agnes and Aga (holding the parasol) on a trip to Nerezima with friends.

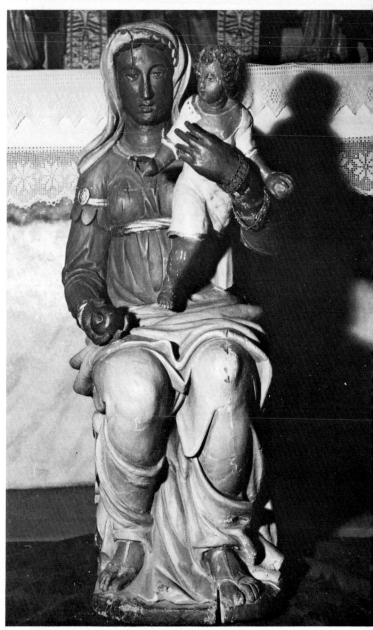

6. *The statue of the Madonna of Letnice. The Bojaxhiu family made the pilgrimage to the shrine in Letnice every year.*

7. *A school graduation-day portrait of Agnes (centre), 1928.*

8. A photograph given to her aunt in September 1928, just before she left for Ireland, with the note, 'Dear Aunty, to remember me'.

Agnes often acted as his interpreter, and she also joined in the activities he arranged for the young people.

By the time she was fourteen years old, Agnes, who had been a regular churchgoer since she had been old enough to be taken to the services, was committed to the life of her church and was helping in a number of ways. But her involvement in church activities took an exciting leap forward and increased when in 1924 Fr Franjo Jambrekovich arrived in the parish.

Jambrekovich was a good friend to the Albanian community, and Agnes's services as translator were no longer needed; but there were plenty of other things to occupy her. He established the Sodality of the Sisters of Mary (a Christian society for girls), and Agnes became one of its first members. Another of his projects was a mixed Catholic youth group, which had a programme of parties, cultural meetings, concerts, walks, outings and other activities.

The young people of Skopje responded enthusiastically to the new priest's arrival. The church became a focal point for the spiritual and cultural life of Skopje youth, and in Jambrekovich's work the small local Catholic community found a new direction. The groundwork of Mjeda, Glasnovic and Zadrima was bearing fruit.

The government of the day was opposed to the expansion of the Church, and rumour had it that it was particularly concerned about the activities of the new priest in Skopje. There were fears locally that he would be removed from the parish. Whether or not that was in fact the case, he made such an impact on parishioners and fellow priests alike that he is still remembered today with respect and affection among those he ministered to and those who worked at his side.

One of Jambrekovich's enthusiasms was for foreign missions. Prayers for the work of missionaries were said regularly in the church, and by organizing collections he encouraged his small congregation to give regularly and so to become involved at a practical level. He gave sermons and talks to young people about the work of the mission field and the great need for work among the poor and the lepers.

Agnes's sense of vocation was given direction by Jambrekovich's tireless work for the missionary cause. She devoured the Catholic magazines and newspapers which he distributed in the church. One in particular, the magazine *Catholic Missions*, contained regular reports from Croatian and Slovene missionaries working in Calcutta. Those who knew her as a teenager have said that the magazine was an inspiration to Agnes; it fired her enthusiasm and developed her vocation.

In the life of the church she found a focus for her own life and also a direction. When her father had been alive, the dominating activity, according to his son, was politics. After his death the family was nourished by its faith. The services, the liturgy, the exciting stories of missionary work and the accounts of what was happening in the distant mission stations, all shaped the world in which they lived; and, too, they were shaping the character of Agnes Bojaxhiu.

# 4

# A CHILD OF GOD

What was Mother Teresa like as a child? And what did her contemporaries think of her?

One common thread can be traced in the various comments that have been made by those who knew her well. Though she was a child of striking looks – with large, luminous eyes and an expression of habitual tranquillity emphasized by her slight figure – she was, as her brother Lazar remembers, a 'normal child', if a little introspective and withdrawn. She was very gifted academically, and was generous in helping slower classmates. Even in primary school she was a bright pupil, and in secondary school she was always at the top of her class.

She grew up with an artistic background. The whole family was musical. Singing, playing instruments and entertaining guests with impromptu concerts were everyday pleasures. Kole belonged to a local musical group which called itself 'The Voice of the Mountains'. Agnes and Aga joined the church choir and were considered two of the best voices. They were known as 'the church's two nightingales': Aga a contralto and Agnes a soprano. They performed at the charity concerts that took place almost every month.

Agnes had a reputation for punctuality at rehearsals,

and cheerfulness. 'She took part in all the events put on by the young Catholics,' a local musician and distinguished composer – related to the Bojaxhiu family – has said. 'Acting, singing, playing instruments, producing ... I taught her to play the mandoline; she learned quickly and became a good player.'

She was also passionately fond of poetry. She wrote poems herself, and read them to others.

Her circle of girl friends was large and she was relaxed and easygoing with them, but she was shy when with boys and needed time to overcome her diffidence. Differences of religion, language or nationality never stood in the way of her friendships. 'She was the sort of person everyone liked to be with – especially the girls,' a contemporary recalled. 'She was a born organizer. With Father Jambrekovich she was our driving force and our inspiration. I still have some of the programmes printed at the time, with her name prominent on them.'

At home she was much loved. Her brother remembered: 'I never heard her refuse to do anything for our parents. Often Mother said to me, "Follow Agnes's example, even though she is younger than you."' In a different family that might have led to favouritism and resentment, but not so with the Bojaxhius. Her mother was a firm believer in routine chores and daily discipline, and each evening Lazar and Agnes had to take turns in cleaning the family's shoes. Lazar often asked Agnes to do his share, and she agreed. If she discovered him doing anything wrong, she never told tales.

She was very close to her mother. Drana once contemplated her gifted daughter and remarked, out of her hearing, that she would probably not have her company for very long; either she would lose her because of her fragile health, or Agnes would consecrate herself to God.

The children grew older. When Agnes was a student at the state school and Aga was at a commercial college studying economics, news came that Lazar had been awarded the Sabri Qytezi prize, which carried with it a scholarship to study for a year in Austria. So in 1923, Lazar, the only male member of the family, became the first to leave it.

When he returned to Skopje, Agnes was fourteen years old. He came home on a Sunday and Aga and Agnes persuaded him to sit with them in the church choir. During the service they sang a duet. It was the first time that he had heard them singing together in public.

The following year Lazar left home again; he obtained a place in the Military Academy of Tirana, in Albania. It was hard for Drana to come to terms with losing him. But there was another kind of loss to come; and that was Agnes's decision to follow God's call and enter a convent.

Drana had known for a long time that her daughter had a strong sense of religious vocation. Mother Teresa herself has said that her first desire to belong completely to God came to her when she was twelve years old. 'For six years I thought and prayed about it,' she said. 'Sometimes I doubted that I had a vocation at all. ... But in the end I had the assurance that God really was calling me. Our Lady of Letnice helped me to understand this.'

Agnes always saw her vocation as something connected with the missions. The words of a missionary working in India made a profound impression on her: 'Each person has a road to follow that is his own, and he must follow that road.'

At the time, there was a great movement in the Catholic Church for the expansion of the Kingdom of Christ through mission. A succession of three popes, each with a common vision for missionary expansion, brought about a revolution in the Church which lasted from 1915 to 1960. The revolution was in the training and ordination of indigenous priests in foreign countries, and expansion in this area was an almost complete reversal of earlier Vatican policies which had favoured sending white European priests into the mission field and making relatively little attempt to generate an indigenous clergy.

Father Jambrekovich's enthusiasm for missions reflected this movement, which at the time was receiving great encouragement from the writings of Pope Pius XI. Agnes also learned about missions from Christian magazines which carried reports and articles by Catholics serving in the mission field. In India, in the delta of the Ganges south of Calcutta, some Yugoslav Jesuits were working, and they sent news home; and news of other missionary activities in Bengal and Darjeeling came from a theology student in Kurseong who wrote numerous letters to friends in Yugoslavia.

When missionaries visited Skopje, Agnes loved meeting them and hearing their accounts of what they were doing in countries far away from her home. On one occasion a Jesuit missionary unrolled a large map in the church, on which were marked the locations of all the missions. Agnes impressed everyone with her knowledge of the details of the work being done in each place, and of the people involved.

But the years of waiting were in part years of uncertainty. It was difficult for a schoolgirl to be sure that an inner conviction – that she was being called to consecrate her future life entirely to God – was to be trusted. Before she came to the conclusion that she had in truth received a call from him to do so, she tried to put the thought out of her mind completely and concentrate on other things, in the hope that by doing so she would clarify her mind one way or another.

Mother Teresa has said little about that period of her life, apart from describing the wrench of parting from an exceptionally happy family home. That parting must have been all the more painful when the course that lay ahead involved putting aside all hopes of ever living in such an environment again: marriage, children, a home in which these could flourish – these were the very things that must be renounced for ever on entering a religious order.

Besides that choice, which was difficult enough, there was the prospect of abandoning any career hopes and opportunities of further developing her considerable artistic gifts. From early childhood she had dreamed of being a teacher. She also had hopes of working in writing or music; she loved both, and had talents in both fields. To receive a vocation for the religious life meant that these hopes would also have to be laid aside, and though she later found unexpected scope for satisfying them in the mission field, she had no idea that such would be the case while she was still in Skopje.

Her early education had been at a convent, but her

secondary education was at the local state school. For all that time, however, she had been receiving spiritual guidance and teaching from her family and her church, and her vocation did not leave her, though there were certainly obstacles and discouragements.

Eventually she decided that she ought to test her call by seeking guidance and counselling from those who knew her best. She began by approaching her family. When she told her mother that she felt that God was calling her to a life given completely to him, Drana reacted characteristically. At first she was careful not to be over-enthusiastic; she knew that the hearts and minds of young children are easily swayed by emotion and religious enthusiasm. But when she was reassured that Agnes was really serious, she encouraged her with the advice, 'My daughter, if you begin something, begin it wholeheartedly. Otherwise, don't begin it at all.'

Agnes also confided in Aga, in some of her close schoolfriends, and in the priests. She has described how she went to her Father Confessor one day. 'How can I know whether God really is calling me,' she asked him, 'and if so, what is he calling me to?'

'You can know by how you feel about it,' the priest replied. 'If the thought that God may be calling you to serve him and your neighbour makes you happy, then that may be the very best proof of the genuineness of your vocation. Joy that comes from the depths of your being is like a compass, by which you can tell what direction your life should follow. That is the case even when the road you must take is a difficult one.'

The firm decision to enter a religious Order came

when Agnes was in her late teens. In the two years before she became a nun, Agnes spent a total of two months at Letnice and took part in a number of retreats. Then she asked her advisers how best to arrange for going to India. She was told that she should apply to join the Order of Loreto Nuns, whose missionaries were working in Bengal. The proper procedures would have to be followed. She would have to seek admission to the Order, go to the Mother House in Dublin, learn English and receive training. Agnes made her application and told her family and friends what she had done.

Many of them were surprised, though a handful had been expecting the news. One who was very taken aback by the announcement was her brother Lazar, who in 1928 had just graduated from the Military Academy in Albania. He enlisted in the army of the newly-crowned King Zog, who as Ahmed Zoghu had for the past three years presided over the republic.

Lazar by that time had been away from Skopje for several years and had no idea that his sister's plans had progressed so far. When he heard that she had decided to become a nun he wrote to her immediately. How could she do such a thing? Did she know what she was doing – sacrificing herself for the rest of her life, burying herself alive in the middle of nowhere?

The young Second Lieutenant Bojaxhiu, still flushed with the pride of graduation, never forgot the reply he received. 'You think you are important,' wrote Agnes, 'because you are an officer serving a king of two million subjects. But I am serving the King of the whole world! Which of us do you think is in the better place?' Lazar thought about the matter for some time and conceded that the decision his sister had made was not such a strange one after all.

Drana's response to her daughter's decision was also cautious, but for more considered reasons. Her reaction was somewhat discouraging, and she would not give her consent immediately. It was not because she disapproved of Agnes's desire to become a nun, but because she wanted to be absolutely sure that the vocation was a genuine one and given by God. Eventually Agnes won her mother over. She remembered Drana's advice for the rest of her life: 'Well, daughter, go with my blessing. But strive to live only all for God and for Jesus Christ!'

'If I had been unfaithful to my vocation, if I had changed my mind later on,' Mother Teresa has said, 'she would have condemned me, and so would God. One day she will ask me: "My daughter, did you live only all for God?"'

So on the Feast of the Assumption in 1928, Agnes joined the pilgrimage to Letnice for the last time. At the shrine of the Madonna she prayed for blessing. Then she returned to Skopje to prepare for her journey and say her goodbyes.

# 5

# LEAVING SKOPJE

The departure of Agnes Bojaxhiu from Skopje was marked by a solemn paschal feast. An order of service was printed for this, which bore the single word 'Farewell'.

Everything had been finalized. The Loreto Order had accepted her application. Nothing remained but farewells.

On the day she was due to leave, 25 September 1928, the young people of the parish gathered in the evening at the family's home in Vlaska Street. They came to talk, sing and spend a few hours with her. It was an emotional time for all of them, but especially, of course, for Drana Bojaxhiu.

Everyone had brought presents for Agnes as mementoes or as expressions of thanks for what she had been to them. Lorenz Antoni, the composer who had helped her in her musical activities and had watched her artistic gifts develop over several years, presented her with a gold fountain pen.

The next day, her friends and family gathered to see her off. A large number of others came to be with them: children, teenagers, most of the parish, and friends from school. Later, Lorenz Antoni recorded the day's events in his diary:

I woke early. First I went to the church, then to the station, where I bought three tickets to Zagreb for Drana, Aga and Ganxhe. ... At the station everyone was crying, even Ganxhe, though she had said earlier that she would not do so. Even I nearly wept, at the thought of losing a close friend. No one could take their eyes off her. Silent questions and unspoken thoughts were running through our minds. What was going to become of Ganxhe, this girl who was leaving for India, going to a strange land far away?

When it was time to leave, she shook my hand firmly. I deliberately adopted a rather formal attitude, to make it easier for her to come to terms with her distress.

The train began to move. On the platform we stood waving our handkerchiefs, and she waved back as long as we could see her. The distant sunlight illuminated her briefly, and she seemed to us like the moon slowly vanishing in the light of day; growing smaller and smaller, still waving, still vanishing. And then we saw her no more.

*Catholic Missions*, the periodical which had played a major part in encouraging Agnes in her vocation, reported her departure in its final issue of 1928:

Ganxhe Bojaxhiu is an Albanian born in Skopje, to whom God's call came while she was still at school. Just as St Peter immediately left his nets behind him, so Ganxhe left her books and set off in the name of God. Everyone was surprised, because she was top of her class and much admired. She was the life and soul of the Catholic girls' activities and the church choir, and it was generally acknowledged that her departure would leave an enormous gap. When she left Skopje, about a hundred people were at the station to see her off. They were all in tears and greatly moved.

She stayed in Zagreb for almost three weeks, waiting for the arrival of another girl, Betika Kajnc, who had also been accepted for the Order. When Betika arrived, Agnes, having said her final goodbyes to her family, left Zagreb with her.

It was a long, uncomfortable train journey across Austria, Switzerland and France. Then they crossed the Channel, travelled to London and finally sailed to Ireland.

Agnes was met in Dublin by the Mother Superior and two Sisters of the Loreto nuns.

The Loreto Sisters are the Irish branch of the Institute of the Blessed Virgin Mary, an Order that goes back to the seventeenth century. It was founded in 1609 in Europe by Mary Ward, a Yorkshire woman who had gone to Flanders because of the persecution of English Catholics. Emigration was her only chance of following her vocation. She requested exemption from enclosure, because she wanted to be of maximum use to the poor who needed help.

Mary Ward was an unconventional and spirited woman, whose radical views and methods were 200 years ahead of her time. In 1631 her Institute was suppressed, her houses closed and her Sisters dispersed. However, she was allowed to open a school in Rome, because Pope Urban VIII was sympathetic to her work. Soon Sisters came to work with her. In 1639 she returned to London and opened a school. Later, she moved to York and in 1645 she died.

Forty years later a young contemporary founded a Convent of the Institute in York. In Ireland Catholics were still persecuted, and over the following years many Irish girls came to York to be educated. Among them was Frances Ball, who later entered the Order as Sister Mary Teresa. When the Archbishop of Dublin, concerned to provide a good education for his flock, asked the Bar Convent to establish a foundation in his diocese, the Mother Superior decided that rather than further deplete the already small number of Sisters she would train and prepare Sister Mary Teresa for the work.

From small beginnings the school's work grew until, in 1822, the Archbishop provided the Sisters with Rath-farnham House. This they called Loreto Abbey after the Holy House in Loreto, Italy which tradition claims to be the actual, transported Holy House of Jesus in Nazareth.

Such was the rapid expansion of the Loreto Order that in 1841 it was asked to establish a foundation in Calcutta. In India it continued to expand, setting up schools and medical services, and today well over 7,000 children are being taught by Loreto Sisters.

Agnes stayed at Rathfarnham for several months. It was a time of preparation. She spent her time studying the English language and learning something of the history of the Institute. It was her first experience of life in a religious house, and for the first time she wore the novice's habit: it was the visible symbol of the beginning of her new life of separation and service. A further symbol was that she adopted a new name: Ganxhe Agnes

Bojaxhiu became Sister Mary Teresa of the Child Jesus. Betika, her travelling companion since Yugoslavia, took the name Mary Magdalene.

The time finally came for them to leave for India. Obtaining the necessary travel documents from the authorities was a complicated business, but on 1 December 1928 their ship, the *Marcha*, set sail. The voyage was long and exhausting, with the ship often rolling and tossing in heavy seas. Apart from three Franciscan missionary nuns, all the other passengers were Anglicans; and as there was no Catholic priest on board, they were unable to attend Mass until the ship reached Port Said.

While at sea they celebrated Christmas on board, improvising a small crib out of paper and singing Christmas carols. At midnight they were joined by the Franciscan nuns, and they sang the *Gloria* together, said the Rosary, and ended with *Adeste Fideles*. There was a wonderful view from the deck. The moonlight shone across the black ocean and the stars glittered in the depths of the night. The only thing that diminished the happiness of the two girls was the fact that in the absence of a priest they had neither heard Christmas Mass nor been able to make their Communion.

Teresa's presence in the mission field owed much to the letters she had read from missionaries when she was younger. From the very beginning of her new life she was herself a regular and enthusiastic letter-writer. In the first that she wrote to *Catholic Missions*, on 6 January 1929, Teresa described their arrival in India, her 'land of dreams':

We arrived at Colombo on 27 December. Waiting for us on the quayside was Mr Scalon, the brother of one of our Sisters. We went to the missionary school of St Joseph, and there in an impoverished chapel we gave thanks to the Lord. After that we went to Mr Scalon's house. We observed the life in the streets with strange feelings. It was easy to pick out the Europeans' elegant garments, among the multicoloured garments of the dark-skinned people. Most of the Indians were half-naked, their skin and hair glistening in the hot sun. Clearly there was great poverty among them. The ones for whom we felt the greatest pity were the men who, like horses, dragged their own little carts along the streets. We had just agreed among ourselves never to travel in such a way, when at that very moment Mr Scalon, who was used to such things, decided to take us to his home in one of the self-same carts. We were all distressed but we had to accept. All we could do was pray that our weight was fairly light for the man to bear. When we reached the house we felt happier.

Nature is astonishing here. The whole city looked like an enormous garden. Tall palms bearing fruit rose nobly up into the sky, and almost every house had its own beautiful plants. As we observed all this, we prayed that God in his mercy would make people's souls more beautiful, too.

The next day we went to the Sisters of the Good Shepherd, who have a very fine church, and among many other things they told us that in Colombo there were some fine Catholics, though living among the Buddhists and Protestants. At about half-past seven that evening when it was time to go on board our ship again, we were delighted to discover a Catholic priest there, also bound for Darjeeling. So now we had Mass daily, and life on board no longer seemed desolate to us.

We did not have a very solemn New Year's Eve but all the same we sang the *Te Deum* in our hearts. Thanks be to God, we began the new year well – with a sung Mass, which seemed a little more majestic to us than low Mass.

We reached Madras that same evening at nightfall. Already the shore presented a sad spectacle of these poor people. When next day we visited the city, we were shocked to the depths of our beings by their indescribable poverty. Many families live in the streets, along the city walls, even in places thronged with people. Day and night they live in the open on mats they have made from large palm leaves – or, often, on the bare ground. They are all virtually naked, wearing at best a ragged loincloth. On their arms and legs they wear very thin bracelets, and ornaments in their noses and ears. On their foreheads they have markings, which have a religious significance.

As we went along the street we came across one family gathered around a dead relative, wrapped in worn red rags, strewn with yellow flowers, his face painted in coloured stripes. It was a horrifying sight. If our people could only see all this, they would stop grumbling about their own misfortunes and offer up thanks to God for blessing them with such abundance.

The city is interesting, but its natural beauty is not as apparent as is Colombo's. In a convent where we spent a few days they told us that there were many Catholics in Madras, but that they were all very poor. Even if they were not naked, they lived in dreadful conditions because the missionaries were unable to provide them with much.

On 6 January we left the sea behind and set off up the Ganges, known as the 'sacred river'; so we were able to see our new country, Bengal. Here nature is also marvellous, and in places there are pretty little houses and rows of tents under the trees. Looking at them, we longed to be there.

When our ship docked, we sang a silent *Te Deum*. On the quayside our Indian Sisters were waiting for us, and with a joy which I cannot describe, we touched the soil of Bengal for the first time. In the convent church we first of all offered up our thanks to the Redeemer for allowing us to arrive safely at our destination. Here we shall stay for a week; then we shall go on to Darjeeling, where we shall remain for the whole of our novitiate. Pray for us a great deal, that we may become good and courageous missionaries.

On 23 May 1929 Teresa of the Child Jesus, after a period of instruction, became a novice with Sister Mary Magdalene, her friend from home. It was then that her change of name was made final. The Archbishop of Calcutta, Monsignor Ferdinand Perier, was present at the ceremony. He preached the sermon and took part in the service.

Sister Teresa wrote a long, poignant letter to her Aunt Maria (Lorenz Antoni's grandmother), in which she enclosed a photograph. The letter was full of happiness because her new life, dedicated to God, had begun. On the photograph – which her aunt kept all her life – she wrote: 'My dear aunt, I am fit and well. I send you this photo as a memento of the greatest day of my life: that on which I became wholly Christ's. Much love from your Agnes, little Teresa of the Child Jesus.'

The novitiate is a period, usually of two years, in which the novice is trained intensively in prayer, the spirituality and history of her Order, and a certain amount of mission work (Teresa's Novice Mother was a Sister Baptista Murphy). It is a time of preparation and probation for the religious life, and as such is completely unlike the sequence of events and mishaps encountered by those who live in normal circumstances. It is usually a difficult time, and no doubt it was so for the young Teresa.

A Jesuit missionary, Janez Udovc, sent news of the two girls to Zagreb. 'They are really happy and fulfilled. It's astonishing to me how healthy they seem to be. Already they are speaking English and Hindi well, and they are learning Bengali, because once they have taken their vows they will go out into the missions.'

On 24 May 1931 they took their first, temporary vows (to be renewed annually, until final vows were taken six years later) and were sent immediately afterwards to Darjeeling in Assam, to teach in the Loreto convent school there. Darjeeling lies in the shadow of the Himalayas, and during the period of British rule it was the summer headquarters of the Bengal government. There have always been sanitoriums and hospitals in that part of India, to accommodate those who have gone to Darjeeling to regain their health in the moderate climate and bracing hill-country environment.

Letters from missionaries working from Darjeeling among the Nepalis of the region had first moved the young Agnes to consider that God might be calling her to India. Now she was in Darjeeling herself, beginning her novitiate.

For the two novices from Yugoslavia it was a good introduction to the mission field. Darjeeling was not unlike the countryside they had known at home. Like Skopje, it looks towards mountains: the majestic Himalayas, the great ranges of Bhutan and Sikkim, and the hills of Nepal. But in the Loreto convent, though the pupils they taught were wealthy, life bore little similarity to the leisurely existence of the rich and powerful who escaped there to enjoy the amenities. It was a régime of hard work and hard prayer.

Sister Teresa worked as a teacher in the privileged community of Darjeeling. She also worked for a short time helping the nurses in a small medical station. There she saw the suffering and misery of the people to an extent which she had probably not even imagined.

In November 1931 *Catholic Missions* published her account of a day in a Bengali hospital:

In the hospital pharmacy hangs a picture of the Redeemer surrounded by a throng of suffering people, on whose faces the torments of their lives have been engraved. Each morning, before I start work, I look at this picture. In it is concentrated everything that I feel. I think, 'Jesus, it is for you and for these souls!'

Then I open the door. The tiny veranda is always full of the sick, the wretched and the miserable. All eyes are fixed, full of hope, on me. Mothers give me their sick children, their gestures mirroring those in the picture in the pharmacy. My heart beats in happiness: *I can continue your work, dear Jesus. I can ease many sorrows.* I console them and treat them, repeating the words of the best Friend of souls. Some of them I even take to church.

40

Many have come from a distance, walking for as much as three hours. What a state they are in! Their ears and feet are covered in sores. On their backs are lumps and lesions, among the numerous ulcers. Many remain at home because they are too debilitated by tropical fever to come. One is in the terminal stage of tuberculosis. Some need medicine. It takes a long time to treat everyone and give the advice that is needed. You have to explain to them at least three times how to take a particular medicine, and answer the same question three times. These poor people have very little education. . . .

I have finished and am just about to shut the door when another procession of people arrives.

'What brings you here, good people?'

'Misfortune makes us seek your charity, your love and your goodness.'

Clearly their needs are very real, because such a journey is not lightly undertaken in India. I tell them to bring those children whom their doctor is unable to help, that I have wonderful medicine for them. They promise, and do as they say. I am happy to be able to give them the best medicine of all: holy baptism, eternal blessedness.

Later, a woman with a broken arm arrives. Then comes a young man who has been stabbed in the back by some delinquent in a quarrel. Finally a man arrives with a bundle from which two dry twigs protrude. They are the legs of a child. The little boy is very weak. I realize he is near to death and hurry to bring holy water. The man is afraid that we do not want to take the child, and says, 'If you do not want him, I will throw him into the grass. The jackals will not turn up their noses at him.' My heart freezes. The poor child! Weak,

41

and blind – totally blind. With much pity and love I take the little one into my arms, and fold him in my apron. The child has found a second mother. 'Who so receives a child, receives me,' said the divine Friend of all little ones. The incident of the blind child is the crowning point of my working day.

In those early days all who observed Teresa seem to have been impressed by the same qualities which would later characterize her work with the Missionaries of Charity: a deeply spiritual attitude to suffering and poverty, and an energy and practical authority which enabled her to make her vision a reality. Her brother Lazar, years later, summed it up concisely:

I often say to her today, 'You are like me; you are an officer. You could have gone to military school.' You could really say that she is the commander of a unit – indeed, of a whole army. She has incredible strength of will, as our mother had. She is a conscientious and disciplined Catholic. This discipline is something she has and so has her entire congregation. It is a very austere Order, organized down to the smallest detail, with very precise rules. And she is their leader.

She was very happy working in the hospital, but she was not there for long. It is not known why her time there was so short; it was possibly on account of her health, which had been poor throughout her childhood. In any case, her novitiate was coming to an end.

# 6
# CALCUTTA

It had been a childhood dream for Agnes Bojaxhiu, as it is for many children, that one day she would become a teacher. Probably she would have taught music, language or literature, for in all these subjects she had considerable talent. With the recognition of her call as a genuine vocation from God, this hope was laid aside and she concentrated on preparing herself for her work in India.

For Agnes Bojaxhiu, the door to a teaching career had closed. For Sister Teresa, it had opened again in Darjeeling. The further possibility, that there might be an opportunity of becoming a teacher not just in a convent school but out in the wider world in the service of the destitute, had probably not crossed her mind at all.

When her time in Darjeeling came to an end, Sister Teresa's superiors sent her to Calcutta, where the Loreto Sisters had a large property in the district of Entally on the eastern side of the city.

However great her shock and distress at the conditions in the Indian cities she had already visited, Calcutta was a degree more distressing. Except for London, it was the largest city in the British Commonwealth. In Calcutta, however, rigid distinctions between communities (mainly

43

Indian, Anglo-Indian and Europeans) threw the social problems into sharp relief, and these were made much worse by the fact that many refugees had come to the city since the partition of Bengal in 1905. Partition had caused considerable bitterness against the British, and Calcutta in the thirties was still a place of political unrest. In this crowded and restless city the Loreto nuns lived and worked.

Christian work in Calcutta has a long history. Catholic missionaries had visited India for several centuries, but modern Catholic missions there began their greatest period of expansion in the middle of the nineteenth century. By 1884 there were twenty Catholic bishops, all Europeans, in India. The rapid growth of the Loreto Order has already been mentioned. At the time that Teresa arrived in Calcutta, there were several other Catholic missions working in the city.

Protestant missions, too, had been active in the region. In 1799 William Carey joined a mission at Serampore near Calcutta which was deeply committed to translating the Bible into Indian languages. A succession of Protestant missionaries followed, and the Bishop's College was founded in Calcutta for training ministers. The first Anglican bishop was appointed in 1814 and education was recognized as having a vital role to play by such missionaries as Alexander Duff, who arrived in the city in 1830.

Both Catholic and Protestant missions placed a great emphasis on education. Church and school were closely interrelated. In a country of innumerable languages and dialects, literacy was essential in communication. But apart from this, the missionaries established schools in India for blind and otherwise handicapped children, which made a strong impression upon the non-Christian population.

Entally was a depressed area of Calcutta, full of industrial premises and rough slum housing. It had few of the pretentious buildings and government edifices that had been built in the centre of the city. The classic guidebook, John Murray's *Handbook to India, Pakistan, Burma, Ceylon*, makes no mention of Entally in its 1962 edition, in a quite thorough survey of the city's areas of interest. There is nothing in Entally to attract tourists.

The Loreto property was spacious and elegant, its well-kept buildings and grounds tranquil behind high walls beyond which the Motijhil slums sprawled. The property housed an English boarding school – Loreto Entally – which catered particularly for girls with family and emotional problems. In the convent grounds was also St Mary's school for Bengali girls, which accommodated both boarders and day pupils. Sister Teresa came to St Mary's as a geography and history teacher.

It was a varied task that awaited her, but she had an appetite for work. Towards 1935 she wrote: 'Apart from the school, I have to care for many of the sick, and help ten nuns in their studies – not to mention the university exams. . . . And I have taken on another task; the school of St Teresa, which is also in Calcutta.'

The new commitment involved a daily walk between the two schools. Every day she left the quietness of the walled convent and went to St Teresa's. This simple activity was a very important part of her training, for it took her out of the sheltered convent and exposed her to the misery and deprivation of the Indian city. She saw at first hand, and with her own eyes, what extreme poverty meant.

In fact, to speak of 'slums' in Calcutta is to give a misleading impression. Slums in the West are almost always neatly defined areas, ghettos of squalor which in general remain within their own perimeters. In Calcutta – and especially after the massive increase in the refugee population since the further partition of India in 1947 – the poor were everywhere in the city.

The grandeur of the colonial city, with its broad streets and splendid buildings, was obscured – as it still is – by the sheer number of the poor and destitute who thronged the streets and camped on any empty ground. The sight and smell of such packed humanity, together with the pervasive odour of human excrement, open wounds and the ubiquitous cows that wandered at will through the streets, must have shocked Teresa deeply. The convent had not protected her completely from the realities of Calcutta, but her excursions from the convent brought her into direct contact with the poorest of the poor.

Teresa had realized her youthful ambition; she was a teacher. She seems to have enjoyed the work very much. Although it was very demanding, she had boundless love and enthusiasm, and gradually she succeeded in captivating the children's hearts. At the beginning of 1935 she described her first meeting with her pupils at St Teresa's school and the mistrust she had to overcome because she was a white woman.

When they saw me for the first time, the children wondered whether I was an evil spirit or a goddess. For them there was no middle way. Anyone who is good is adored like one of their gods; anyone who is ill-disposed is feared as though he were a demon, and kept at arm's length.

I rolled up my sleeves immediately, rearranged the whole room, found water and a broom and began to sweep the floor. This greatly astonished them. They had never seen a schoolmistress start lessons like that, particularly because in India cleaning is something that the lower castes do; and they stood staring at me for a long time. Seeing me cheerful and smiling, the girls began to help me, and the boys brought me more water. After two hours that room was at least in part transformed into a clean schoolroom. It was a long room, which had originally been a chapel and is now divided into five classes.

When I arrived there were fifty-two children, and now there are over 300. (I also teach in another school where there are about 200 children, but it is not so much like a school as a stable! And then again I teach in another place, in a kind of courtyard.)

When I first saw where the children slept and ate, I was full of anguish. It is not possible to find worse poverty. And yet, they are happy. Blessed childhood! Though when we first met, they were not at all joyful. They began to leap and sing only when I had put my hand on each dirty little head. From that day onwards they called me 'Ma', which means 'Mother'. How little it takes, to make simple souls happy! The mothers started bringing their children to me to bless. At first I was amazed at this request, but in the missions you have to be prepared for anything.

The first signs were apparent that the promises of her vocation had been kept. Like the patriarchs of the Old Testament, she had obeyed God's call: 'Leave your country, your people and your father's household and go to the land I will show you ... I will bless you; I will make your name great, and you will be a blessing. I will bless those who bless you ... ' (Gen. 12. 1–3).

She described another encounter with the people:

Each Sunday I visit the poor in the slums of Calcutta. I cannot be of material assistance to them, for I have nothing; but I go to make them happy. Last time, at least twenty children were anxiously awaiting their 'Ma'. When they saw me they ran up, all hopping along on one leg. In that building, twelve families live; each family has a single room, two metres long and a metre-and-a-half wide. The doors are so narrow I can scarcely squeeze through them, the ceilings so low it is impossible to stand erect. And these poor people have to pay four rupees for those hovels; if they do not pay promptly they are thrown out on to the street. I am no longer surprised that my pupils love their schools so much, nor that so many are ill with tuberculosis.

One poor woman never complained of her poverty. I was sad, and at the same time happy, to see how my arrival gave her joy. Another said to me, 'Oh, Ma! Come again – your smile has brought the sun into this house.' On the way home I thought, *Oh God, how easy it is to bestow happiness in that place! Give me the strength to be ever the light of their lives, so that I may lead them at last to you!*

So the promise was confirmed that she would be 'a blessing', and one could already glimpse the beginning of her later work among those who are most wretched: the dedication of her life to the poorest of the poor. Time passed. The day of her final vows approached, the moment of lifelong marriage to the Beloved.

From this period, 1937, there are some testimonies recorded in her own handwriting:

One day, just before I took my final vows, a small child came up to me, pale and mournful. He asked whether I would be coming back to them, because he had heard that I was going to become 'Mother'. He began to cry, and through his tears he said, 'Oh, don't become Mother!' I held him to me and asked him, 'What is the matter? Do not worry. I will be back. I will always be your Ma.' The little boy broke into smiles and went back into the courtyard, skipping happily.

She described another incident:

One day an Englishman came to visit the school and was surprised at the large number of children. In two big rooms we had 375. It can be imagined what that means! During his visit, there was absolute silence. He could hardly believe it and asked what punishment I used to obtain such good order. 'The greatest punishment,' I told him, 'so far as they are concerned, is to be ignored, to do what they like without my taking an interest. Then they know they have made me sad. Why beat them? They have plenty of beatings at home.' The Englishman smiled and remarked, 'The children must love you very much, for you love them and at the same time you are working for their welfare.'

Nine years had passed since her departure from Skopje and her home country. The time had gone by very quickly. Now she approached her final vows with a characteristic determination to be as fully prepared as possible.

Back in Europe, Drana Bojaxhiu, having said goodbye to one daughter, had been left completely on her own in Skopje when in 1932 Aga made the decision to move to Albania and live with Lazar in Tirana. Having studied economics in Yugoslavia, in Albania Aga worked first as a translator from Serbo-Croat into Albanian, and later became a radio announcer.

In Tirana both Lazar and Aga were extremely anxious that their mother should join them, and they invited her many times to make her home with them. So in 1934, bringing with her only her personal papers, some fine carpets and some embroidery, Drana arrived in Tirana. It was a poignant meeting. When Lazar saw her at the station he ran to her and hugged her. Drana gazed uncertainly at her son. 'Is it you, Lazar?'

'Do you not recognize me?' he asked, smiling, and they went off to his home for an unforgettable reunion. Drana's happiness was obvious to both Lazar and Aga, who realized that besides the pleasure of seeing them again, the absence of Agnes was also a genuine cause of joy to their mother, for it meant that her daughter had been true to her vocation.

Drana's faith had intensified since her children had left home. They were struck by the fact that she seemed to be always praying, in church, at home, even when walking along the street; her rosary was always in her hand. Also, Agnes wrote often, and the knowledge that she was praying for them was a source of strength to Drana and her family.

But Drana was likewise a source of strength to Agnes. When she contemplated the great step of taking her final vows, she once again recalled Drana's words from years ago: 'If you decide to do something, do it gladly. Otherwise, do not take it on at all.' She had never let herself forget that advice. It became a rule of life for her and later for her nuns.

At the end of May 1937 she took her vows, once again with Sister Mary Magdalene Kajnc. The Mother Superior, the Archbishop of Calcutta and many Sisters were present. That same day Fr Aloiz Demsar, a Jesuit seminarian at Kurseong, wrote to his Superior, the Provincial of the Jesuits in Zagreb. The Provincial at that time was Franjo Jambrekovich, parish priest and spiritual father of the young Agnes.

> Reverend Father Provincial in Christ, I have just come from the parish church in Darjeeling, which is also the convent chapel, where our first missionaries Sister Teresa Bojaxhiu and Sister Magdalene Kajnc have taken their final vows. His Excellency the Archbishop, Monsignor Perier, himself presided at the holy Mass. Obviously they are both very happy, and you helped them to achieve this happiness, since it was thanks to you that Sister Teresa was able to come to India.

After making her vows Teresa returned to Calcutta. For the whole of her teaching career she had worked under the Head of St Mary's school, Mother de Cénacle, a Loreto nun from Mauritius. Immediately after taking

51

her final vows, Teresa succeeded Mother de Cénacle as Head. Shortly afterwards she wrote to Drana at Tirana:

> I am sorry not to be with you, but be happy, dearest Mother, because your Agnes is happy. ... This is a new life. Our Centre here is very fine. I am a teacher, and I love the work. I am also Head of the whole school, and everybody wishes me well here.

Her mother's reply was characteristic. With acute perception, she prompted her daughter to sort out her priorities:

> Dear child, do not forget that you went out to India for the sake of the poor. Do you remember our File? She was covered in sores, but what made her suffer much more was the knowledge that she was alone in the world. We did what we could for her. But the worst thing was not the sores, it was the fact that she had been forgotten by her family.

It was a timely reminder. Mother Teresa was increasingly distressed by the terrible condition of the people in Calcutta. Drana's letters urged her to turn her attention more to the poorest families.

During the years that followed, Mother Teresa was drawn irresistibly to a startling conclusion. She loved her work at the school. She had worked there for many years. She had kept busy, never sparing herself; but she became more and more concerned about the wretchedness of the poor, their facing death from leprosy and hunger.

She could neither shut her eyes nor close her heart. She could no longer confine herself to the duties which had been allocated her by the Community. When she walked through the streets, she stared at crowds of the homeless and the hungry.

What, in any case, had she come to the mission field for? To teach the children of wealthy Bengal residents, living in seclusion behind the convent's high walls? More and more clearly she sensed a voice within her: *Your task is to serve the poorest of the poor.*

# 7
# THE CALL WITHIN A CALL

Throughout the years she spent teaching at Loreto Entally, Mother Teresa continued to correspond with her family. Despite the increasing pressure of her workload, she wrote regularly. As Europe moved inexorably towards the Second World War, the little family in Tirana and the mission schoolteacher in Calcutta continued to support each other in prayer.

They were years of turmoil for Albania. In 1939 the country was invaded by Italy and King Zog was forced into exile. Lazar Bojaxhiu left Albania and settled in Italy, where he later married and raised a family. Drana and Aga remained in Tirana, and Europe was ravaged by war.

Mother Teresa stayed at the Loreto convent in Entally for almost twenty years. During that time she agreed to be the Head of the Daughters of St Anne, an episcopal community of Indian nuns who wore blue saris – the sari being the simplest clothing of the people. The Daughters taught in the Bengali school.

At Entally there was a Sodality of the Blessed Virgin, of which the spiritual director was Fr Julien Henry. His church was that of St Teresa in Entally, and he worked with the Bengali community. The Sodality operated very similarly to that which Mother Teresa had joined in

Skopje. Its members developed a strong commitment to mission and to service, regularly visiting patients in a local hospital and visiting the poor in the Motijhil slums which were close to the convent walls. As part of his spiritual responsibility for the Entally schools, Father Henry joined with Mother Teresa in encouraging this work. Following the visits to the poor, the girls were urged to discuss what they had seen. Some of those who regularly went on these visits told Mother Teresa that they wanted to become nuns and devote themselves to caring for the outcasts.

All this increased Mother Teresa's uneasiness about her own situation. She constantly found herself watching others go out to do the very work which she herself longed to do more than anything else. From her window in the convent she could see the misery of the Motijhil slums, stretching away beyond the trim lawns and tidy buildings of the Loreto property. It seemed that the only way to reach the poorest of the poor was to work outside the convent.

The alternative had been attempted already. Mother de Cénacle had tried the experiment of bringing twenty girls from Motijhil into the convent to educate them, but they had found the convent environment very different from their own family life. Only two of the girls were still there after a year.

The conclusion was inescapable: to help the poor, one must go where the poor were. Gradually Mother Teresa was preparing to make new decisions.

On 10 September 1946 Mother Teresa went on her

annual retreat. It was the most important journey of her entire life. While she was travelling, God called her a second time. She describes what happened as 'the call within a call'; today the Missionaries of Charity celebrate the 10th of September each year as 'Inspiration Day', because that was the day when the first seed of their work was planted.

Mother Teresa's spiritual director recalls her account of that second call:

'This is how it happened,' she told me. 'I was travelling to Darjeeling by train, when I heard the voice of God.' When I asked her how she had heard his voice above the noise of a rattling train, she replied with a smile, 'I was sure it was God's voice. I was certain that he was calling me. The message was clear: I must leave the convent to help the poor by living among them. This was a command, something to be done, something definite. I knew where I had to be. But I did not know how to get there.'

As she spoke, her face glowed with happiness, peace and assurance. I wondered: was it a vision or an inspiration? Did she hear a voice – or something else? In view of what else was going on, how could she be sure?

She broke into my thoughts. 'The form of the call is neither here nor there. It was something between God and me. What matters is that God calls each of us in a different way. It is no credit to us that he does so. What matters is that we should answer the call! In those difficult, dramatic days I was certain that this was God's doing and not mine, and I am still certain. And, as it *was* the work of God, I knew that the world would benefit from it.'

And so it has been. I think of Elizabeth's words to Mary: 'Blessed is she who has believed that what the Lord has said to her will be accomplished!' (Luke 1.45).

Throughout the retreat, Mother Teresa prayed and meditated in solitary communion with God. On her return to Calcutta, she opened her heart to some of the nuns, revealing her intention and the new call. They were astonished.

She lost no time in seeking the support of her superiors. She described what had happened, and spoke of her intention to start a new mission among the destitute, to the head of the archdiocese, Archbishop Perier. His attitude was cautious; but though he did not give immediate approval, neither did he reject the idea out of hand.

One day, when I was visiting the convent at Entally, I was told that a young nun in the Community had some unusual ideas. However, when such a thing is brought to my attention I listen with caution; for God's hand may be in it. If the nun has humility, is obedient, and has great commitment, the initiative might well be of God. For this reason, I gave her complete liberty to present her case.

The Archbishop listened to her in a fatherly manner and considered carefully what she had told him. But he was not able at that time to give her permission to carry out her vocation.

She accepted his response philosophically: 'I did not expect any other reply. An archbishop cannot allow a nun to found a new Order or Congregation at the drop of a hat, as if she alone had some sort of unique message from God.'

In the history of Christian missions, indeed of Christian work from the very earliest days of the Church, there are few great enterprises of faith which have not been marked by setbacks and difficulties. It is as if God intends, by allowing these things to happen, a testing and a purifying which could take place in no other way.

In not immediately approving Mother Teresa's vision – which would have meant her leaving the Entally Loreto Sisters and starting an entirely new Congregation – the Archbishop was merely following the same principle that Drana had followed when she was not immediately enthusiastic about Agnes's 'first call'.

Teresa returned to the convent and informed the Mother Superior of the Archbishop's answer. Soon afterwards, for reasons of health, she was transferred to Asansol, in a mining area 130 miles from Calcutta. Archbishop Perier inquired about her and, learning that she was at Asansol, he asked for her to be sent back to Calcutta, as the matter of her future was still under discussion. At that time too there was a crisis at the school. Friction had built up between teachers and pupils, largely due to the political atmosphere. As soon as she returned, Mother Teresa called a meeting and set out to calm things down. She succeeded remarkably, display- ing such initiative and leadership that her superiors were very impressed.

The Archbishop continued to consider whether Teresa's call was really from God. He consulted Father

Henry on the matter: 'What would you think of a European who wears a sari and wants to found an Order to care for the impoverished and the weak? Can she succeed? Would the people accept her?'

It was a question that raised a number of issues. The preparation for Independence and its aftermath had presented India with a very complex political situation. The impending partition of Bengal had prompted an enormous influx of refugees, mainly Hindus fleeing from the newly created Muslim state of East Pakistan.

The situation was ripe for political exploitation; many individuals, all sorts of political and social groups, and even members of the government itself (under the influence of Mahatma Gandhi) were visiting the slums and promoting various humanitarian and social activities. Everyone's motives were brought under close and often unfriendly scrutiny. In the current nationalistic fervour, how would a European nun be received in such work? The Archbishop was understandably dubious about the wisdom of involving the Church in a new social activity at such a critical time.

Father Henry responded with cautious optimism. Yes, it was certainly a bold step to take, and it could easily cause problems. But it might just be permissible, especially if the Archbishop had in mind exactly the right person to whom the work could be entrusted. Of course, the nun who was chosen might have a hard task gaining the trust of the civil and political establishment. On the other hand, it would be easier with the poor themselves; caring and kindness would win them over.

The Archbishop decided to approve the request. But

there was another hurdle to be overcome. Rome was not generally in favour of the foundation of new religious Orders, on the principle that needless duplication could easily dilute the spiritual and organizational resources of existing Orders. To obtain the Holy See's permission for the founding of a new Order, the bishop endorsing the request had to make out a convincing case and provide a good deal of supporting evidence.

The first criterion that had to be satisfied was that no other nuns should be doing similar work in the same locality. Mother Teresa's request would certainly be met with the objection that there was already an Order working in Calcutta: the Daughters of St Anne, of which Mother Teresa herself had been the Head. These Bengali women worked among the poor and were doing some of the things that Mother Teresa proposed to do: visiting the worst of the slums, particularly those on the outskirts of the city and in the outlying villages; wearing the sari, and living modestly like ordinary people.

After weighing the matter very carefully, the Archbishop asked Mother Teresa to consider working with the Daughters of St Anne. But she felt that this would not be practicable. Her vision was to live among the poor, to share their lives, and in that situation to hammer out new methods and new approaches. The Daughters of St Anne, living in the Entally convent and returning each night to its pleasant environment, were a dedicated group for which she had great respect; but she could not join them. After some time and much prayer, the Archbishop was ready to begin the process of putting Mother Teresa's dream into reality.

Early in 1948 Mother Teresa wrote to the General Superior of the Loreto Order at Rathfarnham in Ireland. The answer came back:

> If this is the will of God, then I give you permission with all my heart. You can count on the friendship and esteem of all of us here. And if for any reason you want to come back here, we shall accept you again gladly as our Sister.

It was a warm and positive reply. But the letter concluded, 'You will still have to ask Rome about this.'

A number of criteria had to be met. In order to be considered at all, she had to have at least ten nuns who had made their vows and wanted to join her; and the new Order would need to have properly approved Constitutions.

But the first step to be taken was the application for an indult of exclaustration – permission for Mother Teresa, until then a nun in a fairly enclosed order, to leave her convent for a time, though still bound by her vows.

In her letter of introduction Mother Teresa indicated her chief reason for making the application: 'God has called on me to leave everything and give myself up to him in order to serve the poorest of the poor in the slums of the city.'

The request was not dealt with quickly in Rome; perhaps there was a delay in presenting it to Pope Pius XII. His permission was granted on 12 April 1948: Mother Teresa could leave the Loreto Order. But she must remain bound to her vows of poverty, chastity and obedience; and obedience which she must now owe to the Archbishop of Calcutta instead of her superiors at the convent. The letter from Rome took a long time to reach its destination. It only arrived in Calcutta on 7 August, at the end of the school year.

On 16 August 1948, Mother Teresa left the convent at Entally where she had worked for so many years. It was an emotional occasion, with a presentation from the children and songs of farewell sung in Bengali. She put aside the habit of the Loreto Order and dressed instead in a simple sari and plain sandals. She spent some time in prayer before she left. Then, shutting the convent door behind her, she found herself in the teeming streets of Motijhil.

Years later, Fr Julien Henry showed the journalist Desmond Doig his handwritten note of that day, preserved in a treasured scrapbook:

> On 16 August 1948, Reverend Mother Teresa is leaving St Mary's, Entally, for Patna. She intends to dedicate herself in the future to the poor and abandoned people living in the slums of Calcutta. For this very difficult work she puts all her confidence in the Immaculate Heart of Mary.

Mother Teresa had a very clear vision of what she intended to do, but she was very unsure at that stage as to how she was to set about doing it. One thing she knew she needed: a basic medical training. To prepare herself for her new life she travelled 240 miles to Patna, on the banks of the Ganges, where the Medical Missionary Sisters ran a hospital and an outpatients department. The Sisters provided a good training course for nurses.

In Patna Mother Teresa found a sympathetic friend in the Superior, Mother Dengal, who was a surgeon and a woman of strong character, considerable experience and a good deal of wisdom. Mother Dengal was herself a visionary and a fighter, having had to apply to Rome to obtain permission for her Sisters to work in the hospital. She ensured that Mother Teresa learned as much as possible in a short time and she also gave her some realistic advice. One day when discussing her plans for the future, Mother Teresa announced: 'My Sisters and I will eat only rice and salt.' This diet was even worse than the average diet of Indians who lived in the slums. It was a symbol of her determination to be identified with 'the poorest of the poor'.

Mother Dengal disagreed. 'It would be a mortal sin,' she replied firmly. 'Do you want to help the poor and the sick, or do you want to die with them? Do you want your young nuns to lose their lives, or do you want them healthy and strong, so they can work for Christ?'

It was characteristic of Mother Teresa that she recognized the wealth of experience that lay behind Mother Dengal's words. She learned a great deal at Patna. The time passed quickly, and in December 1948 she arrived back in Calcutta.

# 8
# MOTIJHIL AND AFTERWARDS

Her nursing course completed, Mother Teresa returned to Calcutta in December 1948 to find a city in turmoil. Refugees had now begun to flood into the city from east Bengal. They came bringing nothing with them and there was nothing waiting for them in Calcutta. They camped wherever they could find space, on the broad pavements, in alleyways, in the *bustees* (old workers' housing), and on the muddy flats by the Hooghly river which flows through the city.

Calcutta could not cope with the influx; filth, disease and death became common sights on the streets. Mother Teresa could scarcely have contemplated a more appropriate beginning for her work.

Father Henry was away on a retreat when she left for Patna – he had been told that she would not be at Entally when he returned – and his first meeting with her was at the St Teresa's presbytery shortly after she returned. From his description of the meeting it appears that Mother Teresa was still adjusting to life outside the convent.

'Do you know where Motijhil is?' she asked him.

'You ought to know it very well,' Father Henry replied. 'It is the slum on the far side of the convent in which you taught.'

In all the years she had gazed at the slum from her window, she had never learned its name.

At first she lived with the Little Sisters of the Poor. She had left the convent with just five rupees which the Archbishop had given to her.

To begin with, she had to meet people, to visit the poor in their dark hovels and huts or in the streets. In the early days they looked at her askance, partly because of her clothes and partly because of the way she was behaving and the things she was doing. Her presence bothered them. Who is this woman, they wondered, and what does she want from us? What is she looking for here?

Gradually they were won over: she had come to them because she loved them. It was clear at every point – when she caressed their children, when she cared for the sick, when she cleaned their houses, when she did their washing ... What surprised them most was that she accepted them whole-heartedly, entirely without self-interest.

Soon she was making regular visits to the outskirts of Calcutta, the Tiljala slums and Motijhil. But in order to work, she needed some sort of shelter. She searched day and night for a building, never giving up hope. To look for such a thing in Calcutta in 1948 must have seemed a foolish enterprise. Any reasonable accommodation was at a premium and what there was changed hands at inflated prices. Other structures which might have been adaptable to her needs were already occupied by the poor, with families crammed in together. For Mother Teresa, with only five rupees to her name, there was very little hope of finding anything suitable. Nevertheless she continued to pray and to search, and eventually she found what she wanted. It was a small hut in Motijhil which cost her five rupees.

The same day that she acquired her hut, she collected a couple of poor children and began to teach them. There were no desks, the door refused to shut, and the pupils had no reading or writing books or satchels. They were naked, barefoot, dirty and hungry. But they responded to the strange European woman who had taken such an interest in them. Numbers grew rapidly as Mother Teresa taught them the alphabet and the rudiments of cleanliness. She gave them milk each day and special effort was rewarded with the prize of a bar of soap.

For a time she lived at St Joseph's Home, a house for elderly poor people run by the Little Sisters of the Poor. But she slept and rested very little, because at night she went about her business of visiting and caring for people. A slight figure dressed in a sari, she went out to the destitute, the dying and the lepers. She found sick people everywhere, in the houses and on the streets. Many had been thrown out of the city by healthy people, through fear and revulsion. Quite apart from her labours on the children's behalf, she had to combat the problem of leprosy, a disease which was popularly believed to be a curse from God.

Of that period she has said that there were times of joy and happiness but also of weariness, testing, and difficulties of various kinds. It was a significant time for her faith and for her new mission, a time when she was maturing towards a life of renunciation and hard labour in which she could only look to God for help. Her conviction that this was so developed out of her daily experience in which God was her only resource and source of strength. From that situation came the following prayer:

> Oh God, you are all! Use me as you will. You made me leave the convent where I was at least of some use. Now guide me as you wish.

Gazing at the indescribable wretchedness, alone and without resources, she turned to God:

> Oh God, if I cannot help these people in their poverty and their suffering, let me at least die with them, close to them, so that in that way I can show them your love.

The school was her first opportunity of service. Education was an area in which she felt herself to be well trained. She taught the children an elementary syllabus: hygiene, reading, writing and sums. But above all she taught them the divine alphabet: love.

In no sense had Mother Teresa rejected her earlier call. She had not asked to be released from her vows. She did not regret the years spent in the Entally convent, teaching the relatively well-to-do. Her conviction that God had accepted her sacrifice of her life to him remained unshaken. She regarded the new vocation as an intensification and focusing of the first one, often referring to it as a 'call within a call', a mission within a mission.

The new mission allowed of no rest. Night and day were almost the same. She was always busy; she was always on the move. She was joined in due course by girls she had taught in Entally who had expressed a wish to work with her and had obtained the permission of their parents to do so. As the numbers of workers slowly increased, and the numbers of those they served rose rapidly, Mother Teresa began to think about finding more substantial accommodation. The small hut was becoming too crowded; the House of the Little Sisters of the Poor was a mile from Motijhil and she wanted to live among the people, not walk into their lives from far away.

The priest of the church of Our Lady of Dolours was Father van Exem who knew Mother Teresa and her work. One day she appealed to him for a place of shelter for her Sisters. She appears not to have said this to Father van Exem out of any particular hope that he might be able to do something. She continued to pray, and carried on with her work, searching all the time for a solution to the problem.

But Father van Exem did not forget her remark and he wondered what could be done to help her. One day, in the company of a friend, Michael Gomes, he raised the matter with him. 'Can you think of some arrangement for Mother Teresa?' he asked. 'Maybe a mud hut, a hovel – anything simple, so long as it is nearby.'

Michael Gomes was a Roman Catholic and an Indian. He lived in his family home, a three-storeyed colonial house in faded Creek Street. Originally, four brothers had lived there, but at the time of the partition two had moved to east Bengal. The large house consequently stood half-empty. His eight-year-old daughter heard the question and made a suggestion. 'Father, the whole upstairs is empty, it is not being used; Mother Teresa

9. Agnes's mother, Drana (centre) in June 1932, outside the house in Skopje where Agnes was born. The house has since been demolished.

10. *Sister Teresa (left) as a novice in Darjeeling, 22 February 1929. This was the first photograph received by her family from India.*

11. *Sister Teresa (right) after her first vows, 23 May 1929. Her Aunt Maria treasured this photograph all her life (see page 38).*

12. *Mother Teresa and two of her Missionaries of Charity.*

13. *Mother Teresa praying with the people of Skopje, on her visit back there, March 1978.*

14. *Talking to women in Calcutta about her 'Natural Family Planning' method, April 1982.*

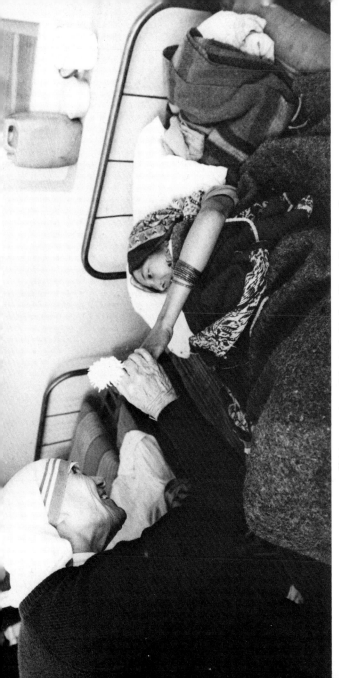

15. *Helping a survivor of the chemical leak at Bhopal, December 1984.*

16. With Bishop Desmond Tutu in Paris, March 1985 at an international human rights gathering.

could come to us.' Father van Exem inspected the accommodation but thought that it was too grand, and he was in some doubt as to whether Mother Teresa would accept.

Mother Teresa, when she heard of the offer, accepted with gratitude.

'It was in February 1949,' Michael Gomes recalled. 'Mother Teresa came with a woman who worked as a servant at St Mary's school, a widow called Charur. But very soon she went off into the city outskirts, to visit the poor and suffering. She took my daughter with her as well!'

As the work among the sick and the afflicted grew, more and more equipment and medicines were needed. Medicines particularly were in short supply. Gomes willingly became a partner in the work of obtaining them. He has frequently told the story of his visit to a prominent Calcutta pharmacy with Mother Teresa, who had with her a long list of her requirements.

The pharmacist glanced at the list, said he could not help them, and insisted on finishing a deskful of work. So Gomes and Mother Teresa sat down to wait, and while the pharmacist worked, Teresa calmly said her rosary. When he came to the end of his work, he looked at the list again and said, 'Here are the medicines you need. Have them with the firm's compliments.'

There was always a shortage of food, clothing and other basic necessities. However, Mother Teresa remained confident in God. The needs were met, and the big house was filled with the poor. What in the past had been a wealthy family house now became a home for the poor. Michael Gomes's life was changed completely. Looking back on her arrival, he was fond of remarking that he had done Mother Teresa no favours. She was God's blessing to them. In the activities of Teresa he saw God at work, and the reality of his providence shone the more brightly because Mother Teresa looked for no praise or thanks for herself.

She has described her work in those early days:

I cleaned the children, who were always dirty. Many had the first wash of their lives. I taught them religion, manners, and how to read. The bare earth was my slate, and the children were happy. At first there were only five, then the numbers grew. Those who came regularly received a tablet of soap as a reward for their diligence. At midday I gave them milk. Today there is a modern school in that place with over 5,000 children in it. That really shows the hand of God.

Mother Teresa kept a diary for only a brief interval; therefore much of the day-to-day work of the early days at Creek Street is but dimly remembered today, and details can vary from account to account. Certainly her diaries would have made an illuminating record of many acts of charity and personal sacrifice, which is probably why Mother Teresa considered it unnecessary to preserve them.

Some entries have survived, however. Here is one extract, which E. Le Joly, her spiritual director, records:

Met N., who said there was nothing to eat at home. I gave him the fare for my tram, all the money I had, and walked home.

70

Characteristically, there is no hint of self-denial in the simple record. It is noted as something quite unremarkable that in a city full of beggars – in which to live a 'normal' life it was necessary to develop an immunity to the demands for help and the grasping hands that met travellers at every turn – a nun already vowed to poverty should give away what little she had.

# 9
# THE MISSION GROWS

Even at the beginning, Mother Teresa was never without fellow workers. Sometimes an ex-pupil joined her, or Michael Gomes's eight-year-old daughter, or a woman companion, but not very often, for it was hard for them to give their help in such exhausting work without payment or security – a bold adventure but an unfamiliar and risky one. At the same time, however, the circle was slowly widening.

One day one of her old pupils from St Mary's came to see her. Her name was Subhasini Das, and she wore the clothes of a well-to-do Bengali girl. She had been a member of the Sodality at the school. Mother Teresa was surprised to see her, but surprise turned to emotion when the girl said, 'Mother, I have come to join you.'

Wordlessly, Mother Teresa showed the girl her own rough hands and her habit. With a gentle smile she indicated the house and the poor people thronging it.

'Very well, my child. See these hands and garments of mine and compare them with your own. The life of a nun, especially a life like this, demands a spirit of sacrifice. You must first forget yourself, so that you can dedicate yourself to God and your neighbour.'

'Yes,' the girl replied, 'I have thought a great deal about it all. I am ready. I beg you, accept me.'

To test the girl's vocation, Mother Teresa told her to come back later, after she had had time to think things over a little more. She was remembering her own six years of struggle over her first vocation.

On the Feast of St Joseph, 19 March 1949, Mother Teresa was praying in the chapel of the house when there was a knock at the door. She opened it, and there was Subhasini. This time she was dressed very simply, without ornament. Her family was wealthy, and for her to discard her fine clothes and jewellery was no small matter; it was a sign that she really wanted to follow the road of self-sacrifice for other people.

'Here I am, Mother Teresa,' she said. 'I have come as you told me to. I beg you not to refuse me this time. I have made a decision, deep down in my heart.'

Hers was the first vocation. Subhasini Das became the first Sister in what was later to become the Congregation of the Missionaries of Charity. She became Sister Agnes; out of respect for her, she took Mother Teresa's baptismal name. Mother Teresa has never forgotten that Agnes was the first to commit her life to the new Congregation.

Gradually the number of Sisters grew. In May 1949 Mother Teresa wrote to a European friend:

Today I have three Sisters with me, and they are very hardworking. How much the people here suffer, and how much they need God! And we are so few to help them. If you could see how their faces light up when they meet the Sisters! Pray to Our Lady to send us more nuns. Even if there were twenty, we should still have plenty of work for all of us here in Calcutta.

In November 1949 she wrote:

Now we are five! Pray a great deal that our community may grow in holiness and in numbers, if it is God's will. There is so much to do.

Working night and day, yet without being overwhelmed by the difficulties, she became a familiar figure to a great many people. At first there were just a few volunteers, mostly ex-pupils, but also doctors, teachers and parents. So her community, or, as she preferred to call it, her 'society', slowly grew. As she later explained:

We are not really an order or a society, but a family. How else could we all carry on with such heavy work, scattered about the world, constantly working in the streets, the schools, the hospitals?

In 1950 there were seven nuns: they included Sister Agnes, the first, and Sister Margaret Mary, the first to come from Bangladesh. Mother Teresa taught them all with the spoken word, but even more by example.

With so many helpers wanting to commit themselves wholeheartedly to the work, and expressing a sense of vocation, it was becoming obvious that the next step could not be delayed much longer – the establishment of the new Congregation.

To be recognized officially, a Congregation had to have a 'Rule' or Constitution, which had to be sent to Rome for approval. Composing the Constitution was not an easy matter. It involved putting a formal structure on to a mission which had developed in no formal way and had operated by few defined rules and principles. The formulation then had to be expressed in the language of Canon Law.

But Mother Teresa did not have to do this on her own. She had expert helpers, among whom were her old friends Fr Julien Henry and Fr Celeste van Exem. She began with a first draft which explained her principles of operation and spiritual goals. Father van Exem helped her in the legal phraseology and in the ecclesiastical procedure. He knew how Rome preferred such documents to be presented.

Some of Mother Teresa's principles had to be modified, for practical reasons. For example, she began with the desire that her nuns should own nothing, least of all buildings; she wanted everything to be the property of the Church. But in India this was not possible, as the Catholic Church and the Vatican were foreign institutions and there were legal problems if they were to be property owners. Eventually the Rule was completed, and it was then passed to another priest for scrutiny and comment. He returned it with the comment, 'The hand of God is in this.'

The Rule is known as the Constitution of the Society of the Missionaries of Charity, and from the opening sentences it was clear that it was the fruit of a new experience of life and a radical method of working.

Our object is to quench the thirst of Jesus Christ on the cross by dedicating ourselves freely to serve the poorest of the poor, according to the work and teaching of Our Lord, thus announcing the Kingdom of God in a special way.

Our special mission is to work for the salvation and holiness of the poorest of the poor. As Jesus was sent by the Father, so he sends us, full of his spirit, to proclaim the gospel of his love and pity among the poorest of the poor throughout the world.

Our special task will be to proclaim Jesus Christ to all peoples, above all to those who are in our care. We call ourselves Missionaries of Charity.

'God is love.' The missionary must be a missionary of love, must always be full of love in his soul and must also spread it to the souls of others, whether Christian or not.

The Archbishop of Calcutta sent the Constitution to Rome for approval in 1950. Several months passed before the reply came, early in the autumn. Pope Pius XII, through the Congregation for the Religious Orders, approved the foundation of the Order of the Missionaries of Charity, with its Mother House at 14 Creek Street, Calcutta.

On the Feast of Our Lady of the Rosary, the Archbishop said Mass in the Sisters' chapel. During the service, Father van Exem read out the papal Bull authorizing the foundation. On that same day every year, the anniversary of the founding of the Order is celebrated.

There were at that time twelve Sisters, and their daily programme was strict. They rose at 4.40 a.m., and there were prayers at 5, and Mass (with sermon) at 5.45 – even on weekdays. Then breakfast and cleaning, and from 8 to 12.30 service to the poor and needy. Lunch was at 12.30, followed by a short rest. From 2.30 to 3, meditation; then tea, and from 3.15 to 4.30 the Blessed Sacrament. Then service to th 7.30, followed by supper, evening prayers at 9.45.

This was the discipline which pervaded the Rule of the Missionaries of Charity – a Rule based upon love of God, love of one's neighbour, and readiness to serve the suffering Christ in the poorest of the poor.

The foundation of the new Congregation was not the occasion for any relaxing of the work. The number of poor and sick continued to increase, and the need was felt for a larger House, where girls who wanted to dedicate themselves to the missionary life could be housed and trained. But there was no money to buy one. Times were hard everywhere, particularly in India.

Mother Teresa knew enough about God's providence by now not to be discouraged. She and her Sisters simply added this latest need to their prayers and carried on as before. She also made a novena to St Cecilia and offered special prayer for this need.

At about that time a Muslim was emigrating to Pakistan and selling his house. Father Henry asked him how much he wanted for his property and was invited to make an offer. The largest figure that he could propose was less than the worth of the land on which the house was built; but miraculously, the offer was accepted.

The Archbishop was undergoing an operation for cataract at the time, but he recognized the urgency and the purchase went through in three days. Father Henry

Mother Teresa to see the house. She said, 'Father, it is too big; what will we do with all that?'

He replied, 'Mother, you will need it all. There will come a day when you will ask where you can put all your people.'

His prophecy was soon proved true as the property, which was actually three houses combined, was put to use. It was a beautiful place, right in the centre of town.

So it was that 54a Lower Circular Road, Calcutta – once the property of a Muslim – became the Mother House of the Missionaries of Charity.

The Sisters treated the poor and the sick on the streets. There was nowhere to take them; the hospitals were full. In 1954, after a series of particularly horrifying cases in which people had died in squalor and in the open, found and loved by the Sisters only in the last few hours of their lives, Mother Teresa began a bold search for a house for the dying. It was to be a place where the dying could be brought, where they could die in dignity, cared for, tended and loved.

Some of the authorities saw that what was being proposed would be of practical and moral benefit to the city, and she was offered the use of premises backing on to the Kali Temple, a Hindu shrine in the Kalighat district. She established there her home for the dying. It was called *Nirmal Hriday* ('Place of the Pure Heart') where the dying were given medical treatment where possible and the last rites of their own religion. Thus at the heart of Hinduism Mother Teresa and her Sisters worked among the dying, and many onlookers were impressed by what they saw.

A story from those days has been passed down: complaints were made that 'the foreign woman' was converting the poor to Christianity (which was in any case not the purpose of *Nirmal Hriday*). The Police Commissioner duly inspected the house and returned impressed and excited by what he had seen. 'I have said that I will get rid of this foreign lady and I will do so,' he told the complainers, 'but you must first get your mothers and your sisters to do what she is doing.' His hearers took the point, and he added: 'In the Temple is a black stone image of the goddess Kali. But here, we have the living Kali!'

If the plight of the dying in Calcutta is desperate, so is that of many children. Mother Teresa often came across abandoned children, sometimes very young babies, lying where they had been thrown on the rubbish dumps, at the point of death. In 1955 *Shishu Bhavan*, the first of many children's homes, was opened, not far from the Mother House. After a while many babies and young children were being referred there by police and social workers. All received care and love, and some malnourished babies made a miraculous recovery.

The community of Sisters was becoming known. Its frugal life and the spirit of sacrifice with which the nuns worked aroused admiration and affection. The barriers of mistrust began to fall, and the first helpers came to offer their services – bishops, priests, nuns from other Orders, and many others of every religion, caste and background. Even high-caste Hindus came to serve the poor. Others came later, from various parts of India. Today they come from all over the world. As they matured in their mission and their spirituality, in their daily work and their communal life, the Sisters were always ready to welcome new helpers. So the new novitiate grew spontaneously. Mother Teresa was its first guide and teacher, and Fr Edward Le Joly, a Belgian Jesuit missionary, was appointed as spiritual father confessor. When he took on the post of Confessor to the Novitiate, there were thirty-five nuns in the community. The following year there were fifty, and the number quickly rose to sixty.

From the outset, Mother Teresa was completely honest and direct with Father Le Joly. 'Please do not intervene in the internal affairs of the House,' she told him. 'Some priests would like me to change things. For example, they have told me we ought to hang curtains in the communal rooms. I do not want them; the poor we serve have none. Most of the nuns come from peasant homes, where there are none either. They ought not to have more comfortable lives here than they had in their own homes.'

She was always firm and straightforward in her dealings with priests. She respected their work and valued their collaboration, but she would brook no interference in the life of her convents. Every difficulty, tension or problem which arose had to be solved within the community, with the help of all the Sisters, and only if there was no solution would help be sought from outside.

# 10
# A FAMILY OF GOD

In 1960 the Society of the Missionaries of Charity came to the end of its first decade, and thereby fulfilled the stipulation of Canon Law which required that new institutions should wait ten years before opening further houses. It marked the start of a period of expansion, at first throughout India and later throughout the world.

Yet though God was blessing the work of the Missionaries of Charity, and Mother Teresa was given the joy of seeing many of her early visions and hopes translated into reality, the news from Europe was a constant source of sadness for her.

Since Lazar had left Albania for Italy, the country had continued to change course. In 1944 it had been liberated from its Italian occupiers, and elections the following year led to a communist-dominated government. The King was deposed in his absence and in 1946 a republic was declared.

In the years that followed, Albania became known as the most rigorous socialist state in Europe. In 1948 the country alienated itself from neighbouring Yugoslavia and became virtually a satellite of the USSR. But there was increasing resentment at the Soviet de-Stalinization programmes, and relationships between the two countries deteriorated.

Albania's borders were virtually closed. It was as difficult to leave the country as to enter it, and it was cut off from the rest of the world. Its relationship with the USSR was almost broken. Inside its borders, Albania was becoming the world's first atheistic state, with massive sanctions against religion and wholesale secularization of all religious buildings and property.

In 1960 Mother Teresa visited Lazar in Italy. She arrived in Rome, where she had an emotional reunion with her brother, whom she had not seen since 1924, and met his wife Maria and their daughter and her husband. Lazar and Maria had named their daughter Aga.

Of course there was much to talk about, with news to exchange and many memories to recall. One topic which they discussed at length was the situation of Drana and Aga, who were still living in Tirana. They realized that something would have to be done if they were ever to see their mother and sister again. Mother Teresa was not entirely without hope, and pointed out that they had friends all over the world. 'Do not lose heart,' she encouraged her brother. 'I hope we can do something through them.'

Lazar showed his sister a pile of letters from Drana and Aga, letters full of nostalgia for the past and great longing for the family to be reunited. One from Aga is typical:

How happy your letter made me! It was like seeing you again. My dear, I love you so much and long to see you – and it is the same for Mother, too. She always has your photograph with her. I am longing to hug you, for us to be happy together again, but it cannot be just yet.

82

You know how loneliness makes me depressed, but just thinking of you makes me happy. Maybe I shall see you again one day. . . . Please, write again. I have not had a letter from Agnes for a while. She must be very busy . . . I am glad she is well; I will write to her today.

Mother Teresa returned to Calcutta with renewed determination to pursue every opportunity of presenting Drana and Aga's case to anyone who might have influence with the Albanian government.

She travelled increasingly as the Missionaries of Charity grew, and the world began to recognize her work by awarding her honours and prizes. But though she often longed to see Yugoslavia – the country of her birth – again, this was not possible for several years.

Albania had not been alone in its political upheavals. Yugoslavia, too, had been changing. During the Second World War it had been neutral until 1941, when it had been invaded and overrun by the Germans. In 1944 the German forces were expelled, largely through the efforts of well-organized resistance fighters. In 1945 the country was proclaimed a federal republic under Marshal Tito, and the government quickly became entirely communist. Over the years, just as had happened in Albania, relations with the USSR became very cool. However, unlike Albania, Yugoslavia tolerated religious activity after it became part of the communist bloc (though since the mid-1970s it has placed very strict constraints upon all church activities).

In 1962 a priest from Ohrid in the extreme south of Yugoslavia wrote to Mother Teresa, and also to three other nuns who were compatriots and colleagues with her in the mission work – one of them was Betika Kajnc, now Sister Mary Magdalene, who had travelled to India with her. Mother Teresa wrote back in Serbo-Croat:

> Dear Reverend Father, your letter has brought me news of Skopje after thirty-three years. So, as you can imagine, it was a real joy. Thank you.
>
> God has blessed Skopje. I think our poor people here, who suffer much, must pray for you and Skopje. I am glad that you are seeing so many Vocations . . . Here, our Congregation is growing, slowly. I now have 149 Sisters.
>
> I thought that the people of Skopje had completely forgotten Agnes, as you are the first to write to me in such a long time. Pray for me. I will also pray, for our people in Skopje, that they might pray for me. My mother and sister are still in Tirana. Only God knows why they have to suffer so much. I know that their sacrifices and prayers help me in my work. It is all to the greater glory of God . . .

Skopje was always close to her heart. In 1963 (a year of great sorrow for Skopje because it was the year of the earthquake), she wrote to some seminarians, students in Zagreb from the diocese of Skopje who were preparing to enter the Church. Her letter began in English and continued in Albanian.

> Dear Theologians, I have received your letter, and thank you for your prayers which help me to continue God's work. I am glad that you are preparing to work at Skopje. Do not forget: the Lord has chosen and called you to become a large family, and this must fill your hearts. We are 181 Sisters, and we

have started taking men – Brothers – as well. I have forgotten some of my Albanian and so cannot write you a long letter. Pray for me, and I will pray for you. May the love of God be with you.

M. Teresa, MC.

The work still spread. In that same year, 1963, Mother Teresa had begun to put into action her plan for a new Congregation, the Missionary Brothers of Charity. Though it offered men the same opportunity to fulfil their vocations as had previously been offered to women, it was brought into being as much out of necessity as anything else. There were parts of the work among the poor which were difficult for women and more suited to men.

The new Congregation was given official recognition by Rome after some small delays, and today the Brothers work in a similar way to the Sisters, wearing the simplest clothes, ministering to the poor and sick, and with Houses in several countries.

The 1960s saw new Houses of the Sisters of the Missionaries of Charity opened all over the world: in 1965, Venezuela; in 1967, Colombo; in 1968, Rome and Tanzania; in 1969, Australia. It was only the beginning. Today the Sisters are to be found in many countries, and in due course the Brothers of Charity also established new foundations abroad; though as a general rule, the Brothers do not establish Houses in places where the Sisters are already working. However, they work side by side in certain situations such as the Home for the Dying in Calcutta.

The expansion of the work throughout the world was reflected by another development; the increase in 'Co-workers', which was marked in 1969 by the founding of the International Association of Co-workers of Mother Teresa.

The concept of Co-workers had originated much earlier. In 1954, Ann Blaikie, now the International Chairman of the Co-workers, was working in a handi-work shop in Calcutta and sought out Mother Teresa. She offered to collect toys and clothes for Mother Teresa's Christian children for Christmas. Having done so, Mother Teresa thanked her but added that she now needed clothes for the Hindu children's party. So it continued, and the group of helpers formed themselves into the Marian Society, which over the years expanded, and received the blessing of Pope Paul VI in 1969. At this point the present 'Co-workers' were founded.

From these beginnings the movement grew until today Co-workers can be found all over the world. They include the International Co-workers who raise money and collect goods for the poor; and the Contemplatives, a linking of contemplative Houses with the work of the Missionaries of Charity, as well as the Sick and Suffering Co-workers.

This last extraordinary development must be mentioned. In 1948, while she was at Patna, Mother Teresa had met a young Belgian woman, Jacqueline de Decker, in the hospital there. In many ways the two women were very similar. Both had received a call from God, at an early age, to serve him in India among the poor. Both felt that the most effective way of ministering to the poor was to live where the poor lived and to dress as the poor dressed. Jacqueline de Decker had been advised to contact Mother Teresa, and at Patna the two women realized that they shared the same vision.

In Jacqueline de Decker's case, however, India was not to be the place which God had chosen for her. Deteriorating health, a number of spinal operations, and the need to convalesce, took her back to Europe. She never returned to India as a missionary, and it was a hard disappointment to bear. But slowly she realized that, far from rejecting her, God had given her a very specific task: that of dedicating her life, with all its suffering and pain, to the work of Mother Teresa in India. In a letter of 1952, Mother Teresa wrote: 'The work here is tremendous and needs workers, it is true, but I need souls like yours to pray and suffer for the work ... '

It became a central part of the work of the Missionaries of Charity. In 1953, when the first ten novices were about to take their vows, Mother Teresa placed great emphasis on the need for each of them to have a spiritual link with someone who was sick or suffering; and Jacqueline de Decker found people in Europe willing to take on that commitment. There are now about 2,000 Sick and Suffering Co-workers who have accepted the demanding call to 'love and serve Jesus not for what he gives but for what he takes'.

On 4 January 1970, Aga wrote urgently: 'Mother gets steadily worse, in fact sometimes she no longer recognizes me. She has become very thin and weighs only 39 kilos. I am well, but everything is very difficult.'

For Mother Teresa it was a year full of reminders of her childhood. On Wednesday 8 June she arrived at Belgrade airport, having been invited to Yugoslavia by the Red Cross. The next day she travelled to Prizren, where her father's family and her mother's had their roots.

She went next to Skopje, the first time she had seen the city in forty-two years. She met the Bishop, attended the Red Cross centre for Macedonia and then went on to Letnice.

She knelt before the statue of the Madonna and gazed at the figure that had meant so much to her. The example of Mary had been a major influence in her calling to God's work; the humility and obedience of the Mother of Jesus had been a guiding principle for the way in which the work in Calcutta, and beyond, had developed.

'Her dress is different,' she remarked to those with her. 'But her face is still the same.'

It was a short visit, with a packed schedule. Crowds gathered wherever she went. For most people it was the first opportunity to see the woman who had become one of the most celebrated humanitarians of Yugoslavia. She dealt with the publicity adroitly, neither avoiding it nor encouraging it, and seizing every opportunity to ask for prayer and commitment to her own work and to present the challenge of the poor in all the world. She also let it be known that one of her great wishes was to see a House of the Missionaries of Charity opened in Skopje.

She left to go on to Jordan, where she was to open a House in Amman for Palestinian refugees who at that time were living in tents.

Early in 1972, Aga wrote to her brother and his family:

My dears, we are the same as ever. Mother is weakened by her illness . . . I wish I could be with you, to help you, and for us to be happy together. On New Year's Eve I shall be with you in my thoughts and in my heart, just as you must think of Mother and me . . .

In one of her letters to her son, Drana wrote: 'My only wish is to see your family and my dear Agnes before I die.'

Mother Teresa did all she could to make a reunion possible, even though the family was scattered and living in difficult circumstances. In Rome on one occasion she went to the Albanian Embassy, accompanied by an old friend who was the Inspector for Catholic Relief Services in India, Mrs Eileen Egan.

'They would not even speak to her,' Mrs Egan said afterwards. 'When Mother Teresa left the Embassy, for the first time I saw tears in her eyes. She looked up towards heaven and said, "Oh God, I understand and accept my own sufferings. But it is hard to understand and accept my mother's, when all she desires in her old age is to see us again."'

The day after Mother Teresa's visit to the Albanian Embassy in Rome, Drana wrote to her younger daughter, through Aga, for the last time. 'Even if we never meet again in this sad world,' she promised, 'we shall surely meet in heaven.'

The rebuff at the Embassy did not make Mother Teresa abandon her efforts. A number of prominent people – including U Thant and Indira Gandhi – gave their help, but it was useless. She confessed her weariness to Lazar. 'Up to now I have managed to obtain everything through love and prayer ... but there are still walls and obstacles that even love cannot knock down.'

On 12 July 1972, a telegram arrived for Lazar: 'Today, 12 July, Mother died at 5. Aga.'

The whole family grieved. Lazar sent a brief telegram immediately to Mother Teresa in Calcutta: 'Pray for Mother who died 12 July.' When she had read the telegram, Mother Teresa went to the chapel and spent a long time there in prayer.

It was a particularly hard blow for Aga. Not only was she now left alone in Albania, but she had been living with her mother ever since Drana had been widowed while still young. 'My dears,' she wrote in 1973, 'I have been very depressed since I was left without our poor mother. How I miss her! But she has left us and will not return ... I hope I can get permission to come to you, and then everything will be easier.'

But Aga died in Albania without her wish fulfilled; she never saw her sister or her brother again.

From a human point of view, the story of this scattered family is one of unbearable sorrow and failed hopes. Even the intervention of influential statesmen and considerable diplomatic activity could not bring together Lazar and his mother and sister, and in Calcutta, Mother Teresa had to accept that the call she had received from God was a higher priority than the very real needs of her family.

Yet from a different point of view it is a story of great triumph. The faith which had made the home in Vlaska

Street a byword for compassion, charity and love, was not quenched by political catastrophe, war and personal sadness. The clear vision which the Bojaxhius shared in Skopje burned as brightly in the home in Tirana, and Drana continued to teach her children by correspondence even when she could not speak to them face to face.

The work in Calcutta owes an enormous debt to the faithful teaching, by word and example, which Drana gave to her daughter. But it was also fed by very real and strong ties which kept the family caring about each other and praying for each other for as long as they lived.

Mother Teresa and Drana resembled each other in many ways, and the resemblance did not go unnoticed. Many years after Drana had died, Lazar reflected: 'Today, when I see Teresa, I feel I am looking at our dear mother. She is very like her ... '

# EPILOGUE

The story of Mother Teresa's work continues, and so does its presence in the world. She has become a world figure, but few world figures have remained so unchanged by praise and publicity. The list of her awards and honours is a long one. It includes the Pope John XXIII Peace Prize (1971), the John F. Kennedy International Award (1971), The Templeton Award for 'Progress in Religion' (1973), The Albert Schweitzer International Prize (1975), and the Nobel Peace Prize (1979). Yet she rejects all attempts to idealize her, and directs the praise and the honour to God.

In doing so, she is denying to those who know her work the luxury of passive admiration. A missionary working in the slums of a distant Asian country can be admired, honoured and financed – at a distance. It is even possible to volunteer a certain amount of sacrifice, to give handsomely in money and even time. But for most of the world, immunized by television news bulletins and press photographs, no longer shockable by the pictures of corpses in the streets of cities which we ourselves will never visit, it is a relatively easy sacrifice.

Mother Teresa will not allow it. Wherever she goes, on whatever platform she finds herself, she turns the spotlight not only on Calcutta and the other lands where her missionaries work, but on her hearers and their own country.

A good example is the House in Rome. It was opened by the direct invitation of Pope Paul VI, who in 1968 wrote to Mother Teresa enclosing a return ticket from Calcutta to Rome and a cheque for $10,000. She was delighted with the invitation, went to Rome, and after some discussion said, 'I am prepared to open a House if there really are poor people here.'

She went to look at the city outskirts and saw the conditions in which the poor were living. Then she went back to the Pope. 'Your Holiness, God has given us plenty of work.' She opened a novitiate and shelter for alcoholics, old people and the homeless. It was situated in the alleyways of the Roman slums, built mainly of wooden planks like the buildings around it. A student group, wanting to meet Mother Teresa there, knocked at the door of a local priest. He considered. 'If you mean those Indian nuns who go round looking for gypsies and living with them, yes, I can tell you where they are. They are a disgrace to the Church.'

Work such as Mother Teresa's is not comfortable: neither for those who do it, nor for those who ought to be Co-workers with them. The students commented afterwards that they had been aware of the slums for a long time, but until they saw the work of the Sisters they had not thought of the problem as one that was in any way a challenge to themselves.

In different parts of the world different needs have

been met. In Australia, the problems are not those of thousands of homeless refugees dying on the streets, but of drug addiction, alcoholism and the needs of the elderly destitute. In 1973 a home for the rehabilitation of drug addicts was opened in Melbourne.

Who, looking at the work of the Missionaries of Charity in Calcutta, would consider their work relevant to London, the capital of the Welfare State? Yet Mother Teresa has always recognized that the West has its own poverty: loneliness and spiritual alienation. In London a home has also been opened for the sick and elderly, the addicts and the alcoholics. When she received the Templeton Prize in 1973, Mother Teresa had this to say:

Here in this great city of London there is so much, so much that you and I can do. The first time I was here in London and we went out at night it was a terrible cold night and I found the people on the street. And there was an old man, a well-spoken man, shivering with cold. And this gentleman would say, 'Take me, take me anywhere. I am longing to sleep between two sheets.' He was a well-spoken man, he must have had better days and yet there he was.

And if we look round we will see many, not as many as in Calcutta, not as many maybe as in other places, but here there are many. Even if it is one, he is Jesus, he is the one that is hungry for love, for care ...

Similarly, in North America, the Sisters work among disadvantaged black communities in New York and fight prejudice and racialism as well as social problems.

It is appropriate to end this brief account of Mother Teresa, which has concentrated largely on her early life and family background, with the opening of the House in Zagreb, the first in Yugoslavia, which took place in June 1978.

At a High Mass in Belgrade thanks were given for the faithfulness of the Croatian people to Christianity over thirteen centuries and for the arrival of the Missionaries of Charity in Zagreb. Four Sisters were presented, who were to start the work there. That afternoon the new House was officially blessed.

The socialist state received the Christian Sisters warmly. One of the nuns later expressed surprise at the number of Christians there were in the city.

At that time Mother Teresa visited Skopje again. She was given an official welcome by the mayor, who congratulated her on the award of the Nobel Prize. She visited the graves of those who had died in the 1963 earthquake, and looked around the rebuilt city.

'It may look completely different, but it is still my Skopje,' she said. 'If there were not so much concrete we could be walking on the pavements of the streets where I spent my childhood.' They were standing in the town's commercial quarter, built over the ruins of Vlaska Street and the other streets she had known. 'I am glad to see these places again,' she added. 'At least for a short time I am back in my childhood.' As they walked they passed the site of Kole's pharmacy, of the homes of old friends, and the Catholic cathedral, which still bore the scars of considerable damage from the earthquake.

She asked to visit her father's grave. The cemetery was some distance out of town, having been moved from where it was when the Bojaxhius lived in Skopje. At the time of the removal, the remains of those who had no relatives to attend to their graves were disinterred and reburied in a common grave. So Mother Teresa does not know precisely where either of her parents is buried. Kole lies in a common grave in the Catholic section of the new cemetary; Drana is buried somewhere near Tirana in Albania.

When she came to the common grave, Mother Teresa stood in silent prayer for a long time. Then she laid a hand on the memorial stone, made the sign of the cross, and said quietly: 'Rest in peace ... '

In her speeches during that visit, she characteristically challenged her own people.

> Do you know your own poor? My dear people, do you know that even here at home there are poor people? There are people who live alone in cellars. Did you know that? When I was in Zagreb I was told there were many poor people. But where were they? Who knew where they were? I wanted to see them, to embrace them, to tell them that I loved them. So with a priest I went to visit a woman in a cellar. What did I see? The same poverty that I had seen in London. There is so much poverty here as well. Did you know? Do you know and love the poor? If you do not know them, how can you love them?
>
> Well, start in your own homes. In your own families, at home, start there, and God will help you ...

It was, after all, in a home in Skopje that she herself had begun to serve God, and he had surely helped her.

The influence of that home, of her family and her

upbringing was to stay with her throughout her life. Even today she has not forgotten the Madonna of Letnice, and though she no longer speaks Albanian easily, she can still sing the old hymn of her countrymen and countrywomen, 'We have our Mother of the Black Mountain'.

When one considers what has been written about her and what she herself has said and written, the influence is very apparent. Several things stand out.

First, it is apparent that the underlying power of Mother Teresa's work and ministry is the power of prayer. Prayer is written into the daily timetable and directs the most everyday activities. She herself has often been asked whether she is ever bored by so much prayer. Her instant response is usually to retort that her times with God are so precious to her that she can hardly bear to bring them to an end. Though she is a very traditional and devout Roman Catholic, and makes use of the rosary and many other aids to contemplation, prayer is for her, as for her Sisters, not a dry routine but a living dialogue with her Lord. 'This is the community's greatest treasure, and we derive our strength from it.'

It was something that her family taught her. In Zagreb in 1970, she recalled her childhood:

I remember my mother, my father and the rest of us praying together each evening ... I hope our Albanian families have remained faithful to this practice. It is God's greatest gift to the family. It maintains family unity. The family that does not pray together does not stay together. So – go back to family prayer, and keep to it. Through prayer you will find out what God wants you to do.

97

She has described the members of her Order as 'contemplatives living in the world'. 'When there are no more poor, no more hungry, no more lepers – then we will retire to our convent and give ourselves entirely to prayer,' she once said, and added, 'But I hardly think that time will come ... '

So important is the place of prayer in the life of the Missionaries of Charity that Mother Teresa has created a 'contemplative link' which spans the world; it embraces those contemplative communities that have linked themselves to the work of the Missionaries of Charity. Other Co-workers, both in everday life situations and in hospital wards and sickrooms, join in the perpetual offering of prayer which supports and upholds the Order.

Secondly, it is evident that Kole and Drana Bojaxhiu bequeathed to their daughter a strong sense of the importance of family life. It is not simply that she loved her home, had an exceptionally happy childhood and maintained strong links with her family even when they were scattered across the world. Nor is it simply that she sets a correspondingly high value on family life as a threatened value in today's society, and has been outspoken on such issues as abortion and morality. Much more than these emphases, real though they are, is her insistence that the Missionaries of Charity are a family – a family which includes the Sisters, the Brothers, the Contemplatives, the Sick and Suffering Co-workers, and Co-workers throughout the world.

It is easy to use such images lightly, and phrases such as 'the brotherhood of man' are often devalued through superficiality today. But the reality of the family identity shines through every action and word that is spoken by Mother Teresa and her Sisters, not least in the letters which she writes to her Co-workers. In releasing her to God's work and sending her out, while still a young girl, from the circle of the Bojaxhiu home, Drana was only enabling her to exchange one family for another.

Thirdly, it can be seen that she was given a pattern of love by her parents. For them, duty was love in action, and while they taught her strictly about the responsibilities of being a member of a prosperous family in a city where many starved, they also taught her that there was joy to be found in loving the poor. And those who have visited Mother Teresa's Houses have frequently reported the happiness and joy that they have seen there.

One does not immediately think of laughter and the richness of life in its fullness as the products of vows of chastity and poverty. But they seem inescapable, both in the Houses themselves and in the written and spoken words that have come from the Order.

Perhaps it is that interrelationship between duty and love which is the most striking aspect of what God has done through Mother Teresa. In her teaching that one person can bear the suffering of another she is not unique. It is a theme found in many Christian writers: Evelyn Underhill, Friedrich von Hügel, Charles Williams, and C. S. Lewis, to name only four. For Charles Williams it was the 'Way of Exchange', and it was derived from the central act of substitution in cosmic history: the death of Christ on the cross in place of fallen humanity.

For Mother Teresa, that is the heart of it. The entire

interwoven relationship of love, translated into action throughout the work of her Order in the world, is the outworking of the intention expressed in the 1950 Rule which is to satiate the thirst of Jesus Christ on the cross. As Christ satisfies the needs of humanity by the supreme sacrifice of himself, so he calls his people to offer their lesser sacrifices in an exchange in which he graciously calls himself the needy one.

It is a fascinating juxtaposition. The Missionaries of Charity seek out menial tasks. They tend the wounds of the filthy, clean the bodies of the foul, caress the unloved; a more down-to-earth, prosaic calling could hardly be imagined. Yet they do it as if it were Christ himself that lay before them. Their entire day's work is suffused by a luminous mysticism which irradiates the dirty and the commonplace.

The quest for spiritual truth has captivated many people in modern times. Hippies, whole movements of rock music, drug cultures and many more have turned out to be failed attempts to grasp a peace and a meaning at the heart of things. Mother Teresa shows us that that peace and that meaning lie not in an hallucinatory miasma, nor in a mindless, depersonalized experience, but at our very doorsteps; in our streets, in our slums, in ugliness and poverty, where clean sheets and hot meals seem impossible dreams, where Christ suffers in the suffering of mankind.